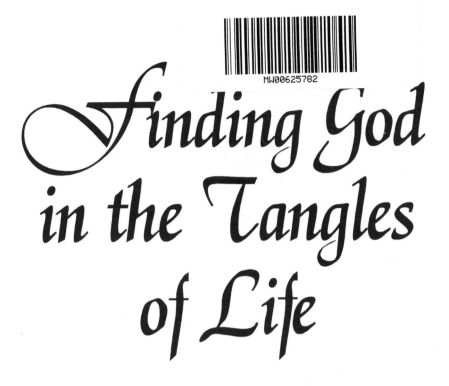

Finding God in the Tangles of Life

Lessons from Ruth

Jean Meppelink

Growing Life Ministries
Box 545
Holden, MA 01520

Finding God in the Tangles of Life
ISBN 0-9657979-2-9
Copyright © 1994, by F. Jean Meppelink
All rights reserved.

Cover Design: Lynn Wheaton
Cover Photo-Wheat: Elizabeth Trask

Printed in the United States of America

Scripture quotations unless otherwise noted are taken from *The Holy Bible: New International Version*, Copyright © 1973, 1978 by the New York International Bible Society. Used by permission of Zondervan Bible Publishers.

DEDICATED
in memory of
Fran and Bess Hussey,
my faithful parents,
who introduced me to
their God and His ways.

Finding God in the Tangles of Life
Table of Contents

PREFACE

My earliest recollection of trying to understand God is that of a little girl looking up into the starry sky and visualizing a God big enough to paint that vast expanse of gray and blue and black with so many twinkling lights! You see, Daddy was a commercial painter. Though I could not comprehend it, I knew it was possible because God "could do anything!"

Where did my idea come from? Parents! A mom and dad who loved God, served Him with all their hearts, and passed on to me their faith in the power of the Almighty.

I saw Him in the way they prayed. Earnest. Fervent. Consistent prayers. I saw Him in the way they praised. Spontaneous. Joyous. Generous praise. I saw Him in their faithful support of the church. If the doors were open, they were there. If help was needed in any area, (giving, teaching, cleaning, serving) they were available. I saw Him in the understanding they gave to the discouraged, the hurting, the needy. I saw Him in the many trips they made to take food or clothing or shoes to a family in need. When no one else noticed or cared, Mom and Dad were there.

Mom and Dad taught me the ways of God. They taught responsibility, trust, loyalty, and love. They insisted on respect for one another and for the house of God. They disciplined me fairly and demonstrated esteem for my ideas and admiration for my abilities.

No, Mom and Dad were not perfect. At times they argued; at times they made wrong decisions or got angry. Sometimes they were hurt and discouraged. But they never gave up on God. They never spoke against their Heavenly Father.

In my longing to know God through the years, often, I have struggled. I have wept and prayed and searched the Scriptures. But always, I am brought back to the solid foundation given me by my godly parents. Gently, the Holy Spirit reminds me that if I am to know Him, I must look at Jesus who is the "exact representation of His being" (Hebrews 1:3).

Thanks, Mom and Dad.

—J.M.

Lesson One

SEEKING HIM

"You will seek me and find me when you seek me with all your heart." Jeremiah 29:13

I. INTRODUCTION: "In the days when the judges ruled..." (Ruth 1:1) was one of the darkest periods in Jewish history to that time.

God's chosen people had finally settled in Canaan, the land of promise. They had found milk and honey, plentiful harvest, and rest from their enemies. Joshua had led them in dividing the land (Joshua 13-21), but they had not driven out the enemy completely. Even Jerusalem was not fully conquered. Gentile nations still lived among them, worshiped idols, and intermarried with the Israelites.

Read: Joshua 21:43-45; Judges 1:19-21, 28-33

There was no strong government. Joshua had died; his immediate generation of warriors was gone, and there was no king. God wanted to be Israel's ruler, but instead each individual did as he saw fit. There were disagreements, fights, and civil wars among the tribes. The people worshiped the idols of the Gentiles, not caring about the things of God. Enemies repeatedly tried to exterminate this invading people.

Read: Judges 2:10-15; 21:25

Judges rose to places of leadership as situations demanded. Tribes were ruled spasmodically and without unity of purpose or continuity of succession.[1] Often a judge's influence was limited to a local community or tribe. Sometimes several tribes or the whole nation was involved in military exploits under the guidance of a judge. Without a political capital there was no central place where a judge would officiate.

Illustrations:
Deborah (Judges 4) had her headquarters under a palm tree and was consulted by Israelites of various tribes regarding non-military disputes. She also accompanied Barak as he led armies against Sisera, commander of a Canaanite army.

Gideon (Judges 6 and 7) was chosen by an angel of the Lord to war against the Midianites.

Samson (Judges 13-16) was set apart from birth to begin the deliverance of Israel from the Philistines.

The Israelites' way of life involved a cycle of neglecting God, worshiping idols, being conquered by the enemy, suffering persecution, crying out to God for help, and being saved by some godly judge who led them to victory and back to God. This cycle of sin, suffering, supplication, and salvation was repeated again and again.

---

[1]Samuel J. Schultz, *The Old Testament Speaks* (NY, Harper & Row, 1980), pp. 104-106.

Finding God in the Tangles of Life

Each time the nation repented, God had pity on them. He rescued them from their enemies and blessed and prospered them. However, each return to God was less complete than the one before.

Read: Judges 10:11-16

II. The beautiful story of Ruth is like a calm in the storm. It pictures domestic life during great national turbulence. It shows there are always those who live for God, no matter what the economic or political situation.

Read: Ruth 1:1,2

A. The story opens with a dread word - *famine*. God's blessing on a country is often demonstrated by the sending of rain; His judgment, by famine.

Read: Deuteronomy 11:11,12; Psalm 65:9-13

Elimelech's concern for his family, a wife and two little boys, caused him to take matters into his own hands. He chose to lead his hungry family to Moab, away from Bethlehem, "the house of bread."

B. If Elimelech had been listening, history would have told him that Moab was not the place for God's people. It was, in fact, cursed by God.

The Moabites descended from Lot (Abraham's nephew) as the result of incest with his oldest daughter (Genesis 19:36,37). Though they were distant relatives, the Moabites did not follow

Abraham's family in worship of the one true God. They had become idolaters and worshiped Chemosh instead of Jehovah.

Another reason God had cursed the Moabites was that they had refused to let Israel travel through their land en route to Canaan. God told Moses, "Don't attack them; I have given this land to them."

Read: Numbers 20:17-21; Deuteronomy 2:4-6

Later, when the Israelites camped in the plains of Moab, waiting to cross the Jordan, the women of Moab seduced the men of Israel to participate in idolatrous orgies (Numbers 25). As a result, God sent a plague killing 24,000 Jews.

Elimelech ignored the history and chose Moab as a place of temporary relief from the famine. He planned to live there just "for a while" (Ruth 1:1).

III. How like Elimelech and Naomi we are! Our problems loom so large we ignore what we have seen God do in the past. We look for an escape from the situation that is causing worry, hardship, or pressure.

A. Famine is a terrible thing. We watch with horror as children get sick and die and as mothers attempt to nurse them from empty breasts. Hunger causes humans to do crazy things: eat rats, roaches, raw and rancid meat, or even their own children.

Read: 2 Kings 6:25-29

Finding God in the Tangles of Life

Every mother knows instinctively to give food (a cookie, juice, something!) when a child cries. We plan our happy times of celebration to include food and use it at times of sorrow to lift the spirit.

B. However, our hunger may not be for physical food. Just as gnawing and just as real as physical hunger is the deep ache and spiritual emptiness within a person's soul. Life becomes a journey, a searching to find food that will still the hunger pains and bring joy, peace, and fulfillment.

Solomon went on this journey. The wisest, richest man that ever lived tried everything (without restraint) to satisfy the emptiness within. His search covered every imaginable area of life .

He tried **pleasure**: laughter, wine, women, song.

He tried **work**: great projects - gardens, buildings, waterways.

He tried **relationships**: slaves, men and women singers, and a harem as well.

He tried **possessions:** herds, flocks (more than anyone before him), silver and gold.

He tried **learning**: wisdom (his special gift from God), greater than all the "men of the East." He wrote proverbs and songs, and lessons on botany and biology.

Read: 1 Kings 4:29-34; Ecclesiastes 2:1-11

Share: Has there been a time in your life when you thought one or more of Solomon's pursuits would bring you satisfaction? Did it? Why or why not?

Solomon's conclusion was that all of life was meaningless - a chasing after the wind. His was an "under the sun" perspective, strictly a horizontal, human view. Because he left God out of the picture, nothing satisfied (Ecclesiastes 2:17).

IV. When Jesus taught us about seeking first the kingdom of God, He used Solomon as an example. Our physical needs will be taken care of when we seek God and His righteousness **first.**

Read: Matthew 6:25-34

A. This earth's so-called pleasures can never fill the emptiness of the heart. There's never quite enough of anything! Money runs out before the bills are paid. Clothes are not quite fashionable enough. A woman is never as beautiful as she would like to be. Houses or living conditions are never quite big enough or as good as we would like for them to be. People are not quite dedicated enough, loving enough, or talented enough.

The lure of something better robs us of the joy of today. The truth is that if God is absent from the scene, nothing will ever quite satisfy. Satisfaction comes only when we say, "This is enough." "What I have will do." "Who I am is OK." "I will accept the people in my life, regardless of their faults or weaknesses. I will love them, enjoy them, and treasure them." Happiness exists only when we stop wanting more.

Read: Psalm 34:10; 62:10; Luke 12:15

B. Elimelech and Naomi escaped from the famine in Bethlehem into the arms of heartache, temptation, and bitter pain. Our desire to run, to escape our difficult situation, is always stronger than the realization of the consequences of our decision.

During their 10 year sojourn, Naomi's husband and both sons died, leaving behind no children and little hope for the future. After her bitter experience, Naomi was content to return to Bethlehem...to her people and to her God. Jehovah was more to her than three tombs in a strange land without the presence of God.

Naomi returned to Bethlehem saying, "I went away full but came back empty." She wanted to change her name from Naomi (sweetness) to Mara (bitter).

Read: Ruth 1:3-5,19-21

C. If things and people and pleasures could satisfy, we would have no need for God. It is the very emptiness (hunger) that drives us to the Heavenly Father. The longing for someone to understand, to care, love, and protect, persuades us to go to Him. The circumstances of life allow God to prove himself as the Great Provider.

Some people spend a lifetime running away from things and relationships that hurt. We can choose to flee a situation, or to trust God in it. We can earnestly seek for His help and learn that He will not turn away from the hungry heart.

Read: Deuteronomy 4:29; Jeremiah 29:13; Hebrews 12:1-3

D. Humankind was made for companionship with God. Without Him we are terribly alone in a turbulent world. Even in the midst of national strife, as in Naomi and Ruth's day, there is a place of peace for those who will return to Almighty God and seek Him with all their hearts.

Peace begins at the cross where Jesus died. "The punishment that brought us peace was upon Him" (Isaiah 53:5). We come home, the end of a life-long search, when we come to the cross and realize He bought peace for us, peace with God!

Solomon's final conclusion was: all that matters is to "fear God and keep His commandments."

Read: Ecclesiastes 12:13

Share: Have you come to the cross for a personal revelation of God? Are you aware of God's nearness when you seek Him?

To Do at Home This Week: Lesson One

1. Read the Book of Ruth at one sitting. If you can, also read it in the Living Bible paraphrase edition.

2. From Ruth 1:1-5, what is your general impression of Elimelech whose name means "God is my King"? Do you think he made a wise decision in moving his family to Moab? Why or why not?

3. Try to put yourself in Naomi's place. Have you ever moved away from your family and then been stranded there alone? Share what your feelings were or how you think you would feel.

4. Do you have any indication from the first chapter of Ruth as to what Naomi's relationship was to her God?

Do you read anything that gives a clue as to her relationship with people?

4. David learned how to seek God in the most difficult circumstances: in the desert, separated from family, or fleeing from his enemy. Some of the steps he practiced are given in Psalm 63.

    Verse 4: He determined to praise the Lord_____

    _____.

    Verse 6: He filled his mind with thoughts of _____.

    Verse 7: He_____in the presence of the Lord.

    Verse 8,9: He believed his enemies would be _____

    _____.

    Do you think any of these practices of David would help you as you seek the Lord? Which one(s) and in what way?

Lesson Two

MEETING HIM

"...knowledge of the Holy One is understanding."
Proverbs 9:10

I. Review

    A. The "days when the judges ruled" (Ruth 1:1) were dark, tumultuous ones in which the Israelites grew further and further away from God. Whenever the people cried out to God and repented of their evil ways, He heard them and sent a judge who led them to victory over their enemies.

    B. Elimelech and Naomi, living in that kind of nation, chose to flee when famine hit their area. They left Bethlehem (house of bread) and went to Moab "to live for a while."

    C. Ten years later, her husband and two sons dead, Naomi is left with only her two daughters-in-law. When she heard that the Lord had come to the aid of His people and provided food for them, she prepared to return home. She realized the barrenness of her life without her own people and without her God.

II. Naomi was aware of how difficult life would be for two Moabite women in Israel. Although all three women set out together, perhaps joining up with a caravan for protection, somewhere along the road Naomi urged her daughters-in-law to return to the home of their mother.

Read: Ruth 1:6-13

A. Naomi's words, "May Yahweh treat you kindly," were more than a casual, "Good-bye, God bless you." Her trust in Jehovah was passed on to her daughters. Her words freed the women from any future responsibility to her and turned them over to God for His care.

Remember, the Moabites were the enemy, and yet Naomi saw God's blessing as extending into the land of Moab. Hadn't He blessed Abraham and Israel in Egypt? She thought of Him as One who provides for His people, and she believed He would be kind to them.

Naomi also demonstrated her belief that God judges wrong. She felt her suffering was a result of His judgment (verse 13).

B. Orpah wept with Naomi and Ruth but chose to return to "her people and her gods." She was returning home to Moab, a place where she was known. It was a place that offered her security, hope for a future husband, and worship that was familiar to her.

Read: Ruth 1:14,15

C. According to Fausset's Dictionary: the country of Moab was a "highly organized kingdom with good agricultural and pastoral pursuits, splendid buildings, distinctive pottery, and strong fortifications in the shape of small fortresses strategically placed around her boundaries."[2]

The Moabite god Chemosh required human sacrifices. Babies were fed into his open arms as burnt offerings[3]. He was depicted on coins as a warrior with sword, lance, shield, and two torches at his side. As the god of war, on at least one occasion after a military victory, he required that all the warriors be sacrificed.[4]

Solomon introduced Chemosh worship to Jerusalem. In order to please his foreign wives, he built a high place for Chemosh on a hill east of the city. King Josiah later destroyed this by smashing the idol, throwing the rubble into the Kidron Valley, and desecrating it with human bones.

Read: Numbers 21:29; 1 Kings 11:7; 2 Kings 3:26,27; 23:12-14

III. Ruth's choice involved more than a casual decision to move to Israel. It involved a new land, a new family, a new culture, and worship of Jehovah. Who is this God whom Ruth will now serve?

---

[2]A.R. Fausset, *Fausset's Bible Dictionary* (Grand Rapids, MI, Zondervan Publishing House, 1963), p. 124.

[3]J.D.Douglas, *New Bible Dictionary* (Wheaton, IL, Tyndale House Publishers, 1962), p. 184.

[4] Fausset, p.124.

Read: Ruth 1:16-18

A. There is only one true God. He is not a solitary Being but a fellowship of Father, Son, and Holy Spirit.

Read: Deuteronomy 4:34,35; Luke 3:21,22; John 14:10,11; 15:26

His name is spelled with a capital G because it is the proper English name for the One who created all things. In Him are found all the attributes that idolatry assigned to various, separate deities: Chemosh - god of war, Ashtoreth - god of fertility, Re - sun god, etc.

Read: Exodus 15:11; Deuteronomy 10:17; Psalm 86:8-10

B. We search to find words to describe God: Father, Shepherd, Bridegroom, Husband. Since we cannot taste, smell, see, or touch God, we cannot know exactly what He is like or completely identify Him with what these words normally signify. Our human understanding of the words we use to describe Him is flawed by the imperfection we deal with every day.

Beyond the familiar words we use to expand our understanding of Him, God is also *eternal, infinite, invisible*, and *perfect*. This is the mystery of God. He is beyond our understanding.[5]

Read: Isaiah 40:13,14; 55:8,9; Romans 11:33-36

Share: *What word best describes God as you perceive Him to be?*

C. The Bible teaches that God communicates with His people, sometimes directly, sometimes through messengers. He wants us to know Him and does not leave us guessing as to what kind of a god He is or how to worship Him.

Read: 2 Samuel 23:2; 2 Peter 1:21

The way we think of God or believe Him to be will influence the way we live. If we believe He loves and cares for His creatures and is patient and forgiving, we will come to Him when we have needs. If we believe He hates sin and punishes the sinner, we will live more carefully before Him.

Read: Hebrews 11:6; 12:28,29

IV. We must begin with the thought that God is the Creator of the universe, and that human beings are made by Him. We understand God to be both *transcendent* and *immanent*. The extent to which our understanding

---

[5]*Eerdman's Handbook to Christian Beliefs* (Grand Rapids, MI, Wm. B. Eerdmans Publishing Co., 1982), pp. 150-162.

grasps these two truths will affect all our other beliefs about Him.

Read: Genesis 1:27; Jeremiah 32:17-19; Hebrews 11:3; Revelation 4:11

A. God is *transcendent*. He has His existence beyond the universe (stands outside of it), and is not dependent on it for His own existence. He has life in himself. Everyone and everything else depends on Him for its existence.

   Read: John 1:3,4; Acts 17:24,25; Colossians 1:16,17

   While we wholeheartedly accept the truth of the transcendency of God, over-emphasis of this truth causes separation from Him. We may see Him as being too distant to be personal. It may be difficult to believe that He communicates with His creation and intervenes in world affairs. God's transcendency alone could never have allowed Him to become a man and dwell among us.

B. God is also *immanent*. He is completely involved with His creatures and the universe. He relates to them in a personal way and desires fellowship with people. Jesus came to the world as a man to demonstrate God's great love and to provide a way by which human beings can enter into a personal relationship with Him.

   Read: Deuteronomy 4:7; Psalm 33:13-15; Romans 8:32; Philippians 2:5-11

Finding God in the Tangles of Life

Over emphasis of the nearness of God subjects Him to the limitations of a material existence. If we see Him as only one of us, we lose reverence and fear of Him. God is a Being who is involved with and near to His creation, yet separate from it. Both *transcendent* and *immanent.*

V. Many of God's characteristics are shared to some degree with human beings. Other qualities are uniquely His and not shared with man.

   A. God *wills*, so do we. God *loves*, so do we. God *hates*, so do we. However, these qualities are not exactly like ours for He is perfect. We are flawed by sin and limited by our humanity.

   Read: Numbers 14:18; Psalm 86:15

   B. *God is personal.* He has a personality. He is an intelligent, moral being who reasons and acts and speaks because He consciously decides to do so.

   Read: Isaiah 61:8; John 3:16; Ephesians 1:4,5

   C. *God is perfectly righteous.* Therefore, He is angry at sinners and their sin, and is jealous of those who turn to other gods.

   Read: Exodus 20:4-6; Deuteronomy 16:21,22

   D. *God does not change*...not in character, ways, or purpose. However, His methods of dealing with a person or a nation may change in order to bring about His changeless purpose. When He declared

His name to be "I am," instead of "I was" or, "I will be," He was declaring that what He is today, He has ever been and ever will be. Jesus declared himself to be God by claiming this same title.

Read: Exodus 3:14; Psalm 33:11; Malachi 3:6; John 8:58; Hebrews 13:8

VI. *God is not limited* in any way, but human beings live within the boundaries of time, space, power, and knowledge.

   A. *Mankind is limited by time.* We live and die at a certain time in history. Our understanding is bound up in the elements of time: stars, sun, moon, seasons, days, weeks, and hours. God stands above the limits of time and sees all at once as if it were now: past, present, and future.

   Read: Job 14:5; Psalm 90:2; Acts 1:7

   B. *Mankind is limited by space.* We can live in London **or** Boston, not in both. God is omnipresent, always present, everywhere at once. Space limitations do not affect God for He is spirit. He exists within and beyond the boundaries of the universe.

   Read: 1 Kings 8:27; Psalm 139:7-10; Jeremiah 23:24

   C. *Mankind is limited in power.* There are some things he cannot do...such as make the sun stand still, or change a stone into bread.

God is omnipotent. He can do anything He wants to do. However, what He does will always be in harmony with His character: just, loving, longsuffering, etc. He chooses to **not** do some things.

Read: 1 Chronicles 29:12; Isaiah 40:25,26; Jeremiah 32:27

D. *Mankind is limited in knowledge.* He puts forth great effort to learn the secrets of the universe. He is ever discovering new information and realizing how much more there is to know.

There is nothing God does not know: facts, details of nature, opinions, thoughts — all are known by God (Job 38,39).

Read: Psalm 147:5; Daniel 2:21,22

E. As wonderful as these mysteries are, the greatest of all is that a God so mighty would love us and reveal himself to us! We gain a knowledge of the Holy One as we seek Him.

Read: Deuteronomy 10:14,15; Romans 5:8; 1 John 4:10

To Do at Home This Week: Lesson Two

1. Have you ever discussed with your children, your husband, or a close friend what God is really like? Do that at some point this week and write down the various ideas these individuals have about Him. Do they line up with what you believe? How or how not?

2. David is known as the "apple of God's eye," and yet he failed God many times. He did some cruel things to other people (see 2 Samuel 11:14,15). What kind of a God did David declare Him to be in Psalm 32?

3. Find out why God chose the Israelites to be His own people in Deuteronomy 7:6-8.

Why did God do mighty miracles for the Israelites? Deuteronomy 4:35

4. Naomi declared in Ruth 1:13 and 1:21 that her troubles were from the Lord. Do you think God brings sorrow and heartache to us? Why or why not?

Can you share some experience of your life that you definitely know was from the hand of God - pleasant or difficult?

How can you be sure this was from God? Could it have been a coincidence? Could it have been from Satan? If you believe it was from God, does it reflect Him as you know He is from Scripture (loving, forgiving, just, etc.)?

Lesson Three

SERVING HIM

"As for me and my household, we will serve the Lord."
Joshua 24:15

I. Review

    A. Orpah did the safe, expected thing by returning to her home in Moab. She was familiar with the worship of Chemosh. Her family would share their home and offer her security.

    B. Ruth did the extraordinary and unexpected. She chose to follow her mother-in-law to a new land. There she would face loneliness and new customs of living and worship.

    C. The God of Israel chose to be involved in the lives of His people. Jehovah offered a promise of love and caring. He is both immanent and transcendent. He is unchanging and unlimited by time, space, or knowledge.

II. God has always put a high priority on commitment.

    A. Ruth's commitment was for life. "Where you go, I will go and there I will stay! Regardless if my home is a tent or a hovel, no matter if I am rejected as a foreigner or caused to live in poverty, I will go...and I will stay!" There was no thought in her mind that someday in the future she could return home. Ruth chose to be identified with Naomi even after death.

Read: Ruth 1:16-18

B. Jesus taught His disciples that to follow Him required all they had. Even family ties were not to supersede their commitment to His kingdom. God desires first place. No sharing of the throne of the heart and no half-hearted commitment will do.

> **Read:** Matthew 8:19-22; 10:37-39; 19:29; Luke 14:33

C. Sometimes a commitment is affirmed by the making of a vow. A vow is a solemn promise to be or to do something. Vows were a part of man's value system even before the Levitical law was written.

> **Read:** Genesis 21:22-31; 24:1-9

Primitive, Semitic people often left their hair uncut while appealing to God for His help in a matter of deep concern. Afterwards, they cut their hair and consecrated it (as a part of themselves) in an offering to God.[6] God honored the voluntary vow a person made and included its practice in the instructions He gave to Moses for the people.

> **Read:** Numbers 6:2-5,18

---

[6]New Bible Dictionary, (Wheaton, IL, Tyndale House Publishers, Inc., 1962), p. 819.

D. In some special cases a parent imposed a vow upon a child before his/her birth.

Illustrations:
Samson was dedicated to the Lord from birth following the instructions of an angel who appeared to his mother (Judges 13:3-5).

Samuel was given to the Lord by his mother Hannah before he was born (1 Samuel 1:11,20,27,28).

John the Baptist's life of service to God was the result of his father's vow, following the visitation of an angel (Luke 1:7-17).

E. The *Nazarite* vow reflected a complete consecration of the person to Yaweh. Certain restrictions were put upon the body to demonstrate it was set apart for service to God. (Hebrew: *nazir Elohim* = "one separated to God," Numbers 6).

The vow involved: no wine or fermented drink, no cutting of the hair (which was considered man's "crown" symbolizing strength, youth, and power), and no contact with dead bodies. With these outward signs being so obvious to everyone, the vow was easier to keep than one spoken in secret.

Share: Has anyone made a serious promise to you and then broken it? How did you feel? How important are promises made to our children?

III. God taught that it is better not to make a vow than to make a promise and then break it. Careless vows, made in the presence of a holy God, are taken seriously by Him.

Read: Proverbs 20:25; Ecclesiastes 5:1-7

Illustrations:
Jephthah made a foolish vow which cost his daughter her life. God was not pleased with this vow, but Jephthah felt compelled to keep it (Judges 11:30-39).

When Saul broke a vow made by the Israelites to the Gibeonites, the whole land suffered famine until David sought the face of the Lord. He discovered the reason for God's judgment and took steps to make it right (2 Samuel 21:1-9,14).

A. When Ruth made a promise to go with Naomi and stay with her even in death, she invoked the name of *Yahweh* (Ruth 1:17 - *the Lord*) as witness to her oath. This is the only place in the book where she uses the personal, covenantal name *Yahweh* for God. She is claiming Him to be her personal God and inviting Him to pass judgment on her if she fails to keep her promise.

B. A modern-day example of the vow is found in the marriage ceremony. God says marriage is to be a lifetime commitment. Often wedding ceremonies contain the words of Ruth, "until death do us part."

Some have taken the marriage vow as foolishly as Jephthah did in making his vow. Perhaps the

Finding God in the Tangles of Life

breaking of the vow is the underlying reason God is so unhappy with divorce.

Read: Proverbs 2:17; Malachi 2:13-16

C. When a vow or covenant between two people is made and then broken by one party, a new agreement is required.

Illustration:
The Book of Hebrews teaches us that the old covenant God made with Israel became "obsolete" (Hebrews 8:13) due to the unfaithfulness of the house of Israel. Because of Israel's sin, God "turned away from them" and declared He would make a new covenant which would include them but would be expanded to include others (Hebrews 8:8,9).

This is why Paul said "...if the unbeliever leaves, let him do so. A believing man or woman is not bound in such circumstances" (1 Corinthians 7:15). The covenant has been broken.

In some cases the marriage vow is broken long before a married couple legally separates from each other. The marriage vow includes a promise to love, protect, provide for, and be true to that mate.   God intended that a man and woman become one and never separate. If one leaves and then marries another person, he/she is committing adultery.

Read: Genesis 2:23,24; Matthew 19:4-9

IV. A home with a loving atmosphere is brought about by committed people. People who are committed to God and His ways, to marriage partners, and to children of the family.

God has given us guidelines that will help us. If relationships are to grow and remain strong, we must care for each other physically, emotionally, mentally, and spiritually.

A. *We are to care for one another's physical needs.*

Illustration:
Jesus recognized the importance of this when He said, even a cup of cold water given in His name would bring a reward (Mark 9:41). Paul's friends cared for him with such things as a warm cloak and books while he was in prison (2 Timothy 4:13).

Touching physically is a basic human need. It makes babies thrive and is their first line of communication with adults. Nonsexual touching: a warm hug or loving pat, holding hands when we pray, sitting close - all are essential to building intimacy.

Illustrations:
The sinful woman of Luke 7:36-39 expressed her love and appreciation to Jesus by touching and kissing Him.

The prodigal son was welcomed by his father with fervent hugging and kisses (Luke 15:20).

Jesus expressed caring and love for the babies and children who were brought to Him by touching them and taking them in His arms (Mark 9:36; Luke 18:15).

Commitment to be faithful to the marriage bed is a basic requirement for finding happiness in marriage. The Bible clearly teaches we are to find all of our sexual enjoyment in one person. Marital contentment is life-giving.

Read: Proverbs 5:15-23; 1 Corinthians 7:1-5; Hebrews 13:4

B. *We are to care for the emotional needs of those we love.* There must be a consistent effort to spend time together if emotional needs are to be understood and met.

One way is to do life's tasks together. Working on a special project or just taking care of routine cleaning, laundry, or yard work together, allows for the sharing of ideas and feelings. Trust is built as we share without fear of criticism.

We must determine to communicate with each other using words that build and support. Unkind words hurt and destroy the bonding process. Silence is negative. Watching television does not bring intimacy, for it involves very little giving or receiving of ideas or feelings.

Read: Proverbs 16:24; Ephesians 4:29; 1 Thessalonians 5:11

C. *Good relationships call for coming together in mental agreement.* Such issues as plans for the future, financial obligations, and the training of children need understanding and harmony.

Some marriages are in serious trouble and friendships often cool because one partner has put forth the effort to learn and grow intellectually, while the other has remained disinterested in expanding his/her education.

Read: Proverbs 3:13,14; Amos 3:3; 2 Timothy 2:15; 1 Peter 1:13

D. *Sharing in the things of God for spiritual growth* brings a sense of destiny and helps lift us above the cares of life that cause division in our relationships.

Reading the Word, praying, and attending church together are powerful sources for the healing of hurts and disagreements. As we draw closer to our loving Heavenly Father, we automatically draw closer to each other. As we see our faults and receive His forgiveness, we are able to forgive. As we thank the Lord for His blessings, we appreciate each other more. And as we mature in the things of God, we learn to work in unity with those we love.

Read: Ecclesiastes 4:9-12; Ephesians 4:2-6,13-16

V. In every normal relationship there will be times when partners are at odds. Emotions may say, "We will never love each other again."

When we are young, problems seem more temporary and conquerable. But when tragedy hits, or the daily frustrations of life pull and tug at our emotions, an uncommitted relationship can crumble.

Commitment says, when I am bored or angry, I will still act kindly to those I am committed to. When I am not feeling love, I will still act as if I do. Love is more than a feeling. It is a commitment.

We are commanded to "Keep on loving each other..." (Hebrews 13:1) and to demonstrate that love with action, not just words.

Read: 1 John 3:16-18

What will we do when trouble strikes? When life gets dull or disappointment comes, there is a tendency to run, to get away from the people who have caused us hurt and disappointment. Knowing Jesus gives us a refuge to which we can go. He gives us strength to keep our commitments.

To Do at Home This Week: Lesson Three

1. Read again the words of Ruth's commitment to Naomi in Ruth 1:16,17. Paraphrase her decision in your own words.

2. Ruth's vows are often quoted in marriage ceremonies. Note the parallels of marriage and the church from Ephesians 5:22-25. In what ways are they alike?

3. Have you ever made a promise and later regretted it? What would you have done differently today?

3. Several steps are involved when we commit our lives to the Lord Jesus Christ. From the following verses what is required?

Matthew 6:24

_____

Matthew 6:33

_____

Luke 9:23-26

_____

Romans 10:9,10

_____

Ephesians 2:10

_____

4. What do you feel you gave up to follow the Lord? What did you gain?

Lesson Four

GROWING IN HIM

"So neither he who plants nor he who waters is anything, but only God, who makes things grow." 1 Corinthians 3:7

I. Review

    A. A vow is very important to the Lord. It involves a solemn promise to be or to do something. Sometimes a vow was imposed upon a child by his parents. (Examples: Samson and John the Baptist.) Other times, vows were made voluntarily by an individual who wished a special favor from God.

    B. The marriage vow requires a commitment to minister to a spouse physically, emotionally, mentally, and spiritually. Marital faithfulness is a high priority to God and those who adhere to it find fulfillment and contentment.

II. Canaan was a "land of wheat and barley" (Deuteronomy 8:8). The making of bread was one of the earliest gifts of God to His earthly creatures.

Naomi and Ruth arrived in Bethlehem just as the barley harvest was beginning...perhaps the end of April or beginning of May.

Read: Ruth 1:19-22

    A. Barley was sowed in October or November and again immediately after winter so that the harvest continued through the summer. One of the first grains to be harvested (before wheat), it brought joy, singing, and thankfulness to God for His provision.

Barley was food for horses as well as for the family. It was considered inferior to wheat - a food for poor people. When an enemy invaded Israel, he often left only barley for the people to eat.

Illustrations:
Five barley loaves were used by the disciples in John 6:9.

In Revelation 6:6 a measure of wheat is worth three of barley.

B. As Ruth and Naomi settled into their new home (possibly the old homestead of Elimelech and Naomi), they realized they had to do something to provide food for their table.

Ruth requested that Naomi allow her to go and pick up grain as the Old Testament law allowed. This was their welfare program. Owners were not to clean out the corners of the field or to pick up what was dropped but leave it for the "poor and the alien" (Leviticus 23:22). Ruth qualified as both.

Ruth felt responsible to provide for Naomi and herself and demonstrated her willingness to serve by working steadily from morning to evening. She didn't quit but went day after day throughout the barley and wheat harvest. The daily grind was back-breaking and hot. She needed determination, patience, and purpose.

Read: Ruth 2:1-7

C. Ruth's diligence was rewarded by the kindness of Boaz who spoke to her, offered her a refreshing sour drink, bread, and roasted grain (all she could eat) for lunch. He told his workers to pull some stalks of grain from their bundles and leave them for her to pick up.

Ruth and Naomi did not view Boaz' kindness as luck or coincidence, but saw it as God's way of providing for them in their need. They had sought refuge under the wings of the God of Israel and He had not let them down. He knew Boaz. He knew the need of His children. Ruth accepted Boaz's gifts with humility. She was not presumptuous but was willing to receive what he gave.

Share: Do you find it more difficult to receive help than to give it? Why do you think this is? What should our attitude be when we are in need?

III. Scripture has much to say regarding spiritual growth. Many Christians remain "babes" or "seedlings" that need constant care. As with the grain harvest, spiritual growth requires the right growing conditions if maturity is to be reached.

Read: Matthew 13:3-23

Plants do not bear fruit as the result of a commandment but as a natural result of the right seed and the right soil, climate, and cultivation. Ruth's example can help us understand what is essential to spiritual growth and maturity. We are commanded to do the things that will provide those conditions necessary for growth.

A. *Spiritual growth requires a teachable spirit...a willingness to learn from others.* Ruth had to lay aside her pride, her education, and her wealth, and be willing to learn new ways.

An attitude that is humble, thankful, forgiving, and teachable creates a climate for growth. Humility does not indicate weakness but rather demonstrates appreciation for the gifts God has entrusted to others.

Illustrations:
Moses was a powerful leader, yet was "a very humble man, more humble than anyone else on the face of the earth" (Numbers 12:3). He was long suffering with the people and willing to live with them in the wilderness.

Jesus did not retaliate with threats or insults when He suffered (1 Peter 2:23), but neither was He afraid to call the Pharisees "hypocrites" and "whitewashed tombs" when He saw their wickedness (Matthew 23:27).

B. *Growing calls for righteous living...obedience, without rebellion toward God and His laws.* Ruth demonstrated a willingness to live by the laws of the Israelites' God. Though perhaps strange to her, she willingly obeyed them (Ruth 3:5).

The person who walks with the Lord and grows in spiritual things, wants less and less of the old way of life and more and more of holiness, purity, and goodness. Spiritual growth ceases at the point of disobedience.

Read: Romans 6:11,19; Colossians 1:10; Hebrews 5:12-14

C. *Growing is brought about by consistent, faithful, and dependable service.* Ruth worked from morning to evening until the harvest was finished - every day! She earned the respect of fellow workers by her diligence.

Read: Ruth 2:17,18,22,23

It is important to find a place in God's harvest field where the gifts and talents He has given are not wasted but used to bless His kingdom. Without an outlet for serving somewhere, personal spiritual growth is limited.

Read: Romans 12:1,3-8,11; 1 Peter 4:10

D. *Spiritual growth is aided by belonging to a healthy Christian community for support, for training, and for testing.* The fruit of the Spirit is produced in relationship.

Ruth lived with her mother-in-law (Ruth 2:23). This included the probable adjustment of living at the slower pace of an older person whose values and ideas were different. Because she loved her, Ruth showed respect and submitted to her mother-in-law's wishes.

A Christian community (church) provides a place to develop God-given talents, to serve others, and to worship the Creator. In the church pastors and teachers instruct the body in the knowledge of our Lord Jesus Christ. It is there that we are challenged to use the fruits of patience, kindness, goodness, faithfulness, and gentleness.

As we join hands with other Christians with unity of purpose, we are enabled to fulfill the Great Commission to evangelize the world.

The one who tries to live the Christian life alone is like a log or coal removed from the fire. It soon cools off and loses its power to bring warmth and light.

Read: Psalm 133:1; Acts 4:32; Ephesians 4:11-13

E. *Spiritual growth requires staying close to the Lord.* "Ruth stayed close to the servant girls of Boaz to glean..." (Ruth 2:23). This was her place of protection and of provision. Here she could depend on Boaz and his workers to watch over her.

Staying close to our Source of provision and protection requires communication with God on a daily basis. Wings of prayer and praise become stronger with use. They are the means God has provided for close fellowship with himself.

God will be known in the daily grind. He gives strength to the weary. He comforts when hearts are broken. He gives peace in the midst of turmoil and joy and hope in time of sorrow.

Read: Psalm 91:14,15; 145:18,19

F. *Growth requires perseverance.* There is no instant maturity. Ruth stayed until the barley and wheat harvests were finished.

Paul speaks of running a race and finishing it, of running to "get a crown that will last forever" (1 Corinthians 9:25).

Satan does everything he can to get God's children to quit...to not finish the race...to leave before the harvest is complete.
-He brings *discouragement.*
-He brings *weariness.*
-He causes *misunderstandings*
-He stirs up *discontent.*
-He magnifies the *failures of others.*

Read: Galatians 6:9: Revelation 2:7,10,17

IV. Growth is brought about by what goes on in secret. It is the result of right growing conditions and occurs naturally and at its own pace. In fact, it is impossible to stop spiritual growth when a person lives in obedience to God.

God is the source of spiritual growth, not man. Paul can plant and Apollos water, but only God can make the seed grow (1 Corinthians 3:6). Growth happens as "every supporting ligament, grows and builds itself up in love, as each part does its work" (Ephesians 4:16).

Read: Galatians 5:22; Colossians 1:10; 2 Thessalonians 1:3

Share: As you read the above Scriptures can you say that you have observed spiritual growth in your own life? In knowledge of Jesus? In love for other Christians? In the fruit of the Spirit: love, joy and peace?

To Do at Home This Week: Lesson Four

1. Spiritual maturity involves growing in the "grace and knowledge of our Lord Jesus Christ" (2 Peter 3:18). Grace involves how we act. Knowledge involves how we think.

   In what way have you experienced God's *grace* this week?

   In what way have you grown in *knowledge* of the Lord?

2. Get to know more of God through the following Scriptures. List briefly what each particular verse teaches you about Him.

   Job 42:2

   _____

   Psalm 18:30

   _____

   Psalm 85:12

3. Review the requirements for spiritual growth given in this lesson. Grade yourself on each step using a scale of 1 to 10 (1=poor 10=good).

A. A right attitude: 1 2 3 4 5 6 7 8 9 10

B. Righteous living: 1 2 3 4 5 6 7 8 9 10

C. Diligent service: 1 2 3 4 5 6 7 8 9 10

D. Involvement in a healthy Christian community:
   1 2 3 4 5 6 7 8 9 10

E. Staying close to God through regular Bible reading and prayer: 1 2 3 4 5 6 7 8 9 10

F. Perseverance. Hanging in when it is hard:
   1 2 3 4 5 6 7 8 9 10

Are you willing to make changes to help create the proper conditions for your own spiritual growth?

4. Many times we feel like we aren't growing at all. In times like that what can we do?

John 15:4,5

_____

Ephesians 6:10,11

_____

Hebrews 4:15, 16

Lesson Five

TRUSTING HIM

"Trust in the Lord with all your heart and lean not on your own understanding." Proverbs 3:5

I. Review

    A. Growing in the Lord is the natural result of right conditions being established in our lives:
-Developing a right attitude: humble, teachable, obedient.
-Living pure, righteous lives, without hidden, unconfessed sin.
-Being diligent in service.
-Drawing support from a healthy Christian community.

    B. We must stay close to the Source - our Provider/ Protector - the Heavenly Father. Growth requires perseverance, there is no instant growth.

II. Today we are introduced to a new character in the life of Ruth, the Moabitess: Boaz. From Ruth 2:19 we get the feeling that Ruth did not know Boaz before she found herself gleaning in his field. It was her mother-in-law who recognized his name as a relative of her late husband.

    A. Boaz was a man of high standing. He was a capable and powerful person whose wealth and high reputation in Bethlehem gave him strong influence among his peers.

Read: Ruth 2:1-9

The name *Boaz* has a probable meaning of "in him is strength" or "of strong spirit". Ruth 2:1 indicates that he was a *relative* (NIV). *Friend* could be a better meaning. "Naomi had a friend," not a stranger, but someone well known to her, probably through her marriage to Elimelech.[7]

Boaz was the son of Salmon and Rahab (Matthew 1:5). Rahab, a Gentile, was a prostitute who welcomed and hid Jewish spies before the Israelites entered Jericho in Canaan. She was saved from death by hanging a scarlet thread in her window. Later she became part of the nation of Israel.

Read: Joshua 6:25; Hebrews 11:31

B. Boaz's nature is revealed by the way he treated his servants and the way they responded to him. The harvesters were usually a coarse lot made up of poor Israelites, foreigners, and transients. Instead of being a demanding tyrant/boss who was interested only in production, Boaz was friendly, kind, and observant.

Boaz took note of Ruth, a foreigner working in his field, and offered her kindness in the way of protection, food to eat, and the promise of future work. He did not embarrass her with questions but

---

[7]Robert L. Hubbard, Jr., *The New International Commentary on the Old Testament, The Book of Ruth,* (Grand Rapids, MI, William B. Eerdmans Publishing Company, 1988) pp. 132,133.

rather praised her for the good he had heard about her. He wished her God's blessing.

This is a beautiful picture of Jesus, our Redeemer, who takes note of what is going on in our lives and offers to meet all of our needs: physical, material, emotional, and social, as well as spiritual.

Read: Ruth 2:10-18; Ephesians 1:7,8; 1 Peter 1:18,19

C. Ruth's response to her situation could have been one of anger, or self-pity because of all the loss she had endured. Instead, she demonstrated courage, humility, and thankfulness. She responded to Boaz's kindness with devotion and hard work.

III. In every life there will be adversity, loss, or trials of some kind. It is easy to see this as God's punishment in the life of a rebellious, hard-hearted sinner. It is more difficult to accept in the life of someone who is dedicated to God.

Illustrations:
Job: godly, upright, and concerned for his family, he still suffered the agony of material devastation and bodily pain (Job 1:1-5; 30:26-31).

Joseph: one of 12 children, beloved, gentle, and sensitive, yet persecuted and rejected by his own brothers, sold into slavery, misunderstood, and imprisoned (Genesis 37-47).

Paul and Silas: imprisoned for casting out a demon and preaching the gospel (Acts 16:16-40).

Where was God in all of this? We search the Scriptures for clues as to why God allows such trouble for His children.

A. Sometimes adversity is the *result of sin or disobedience* in the life of the believer. Sin brings consequences that may have to be endured for many years.

   Suffering often helps a person get rid of sin and become more centered on things that are eternal. As we walk with the Lord, His Spirit helps us overcome temptation. Because of Jesus' sacrifice on Calvary we are no longer slaves to sin.

   Read: Romans 8:9,37; 1 Corinthians 10:13; 1 Peter 4:1,2

   Share: *What changes have you observed in the spiritual life of one who has suffered great loss or sickness?*

B. *Partaking of Communion without recognizing the body of the Lord* can bring judgment in the form of sickness or death. This is not speaking of losing one's salvation, but rather of God's discipline in the life of one who is careless about the things of God.

   Read: 1 Corinthians 11:29,30

C. Sometimes adversity is allowed by the Heavenly Father to *prune the unnecessary* from our lives that we might bear more or better fruit. Values and priorities change with adversity. Although the pruning process may be very painful, God's discipline always has our best interest as its goal.

Read: John 15:2-4; Hebrews 12:7-11

D. Sometimes suffering is simply the result of *living in a fallen world with fallen people*. The whole world is under the curse of sin and all who live here are affected by it. Unwise choices made by imperfect people can cause disappointment and hurt. Someone else's wrongdoing may be the reason for suffering or problems.

Read: Romans 8:22; Galatians 3:22; Hebrews 2:8

Illustrations:
Paul and Barnabas (godly men) had a sharp disagreement between them that caused the splitting up of their evangelistic team. This was probably a time of suffering for John Mark, their young protege. In spite of this, Paul maintained an effective ministry and later was reconciled to Mark (Acts 15:36-40; 2 Timothy 4:11).

Today: Water or food supplies may be contaminated by uncaring industries, causing cancer in innocent people.

E. Sometimes suffering is caused by a *direct attack of Satan* against those who love God or are involved

in the work of His kingdom. He is an enemy and
"...prowls around like a roaring lion looking for
someone to devour" (1 Peter 5:8, 9).

Read: Ephesians 6:12

Illustration:
*Job's suffering was clearly caused by the devil's
vicious attack (Job 1:6-20).*

F. Sometimes God allows suffering *that His glory
    might be demonstrated* to a world of unbelieving
    men and women. Always His goal is to bring
    mankind to himself. In times of adversity God is
    able to demonstrate His love. Whatever the reason
    for the trial or suffering, God can use it for good.

Illustrations:
*Abraham waited so long for a son that the miracle
of Isaac's birth in Abraham and Sarah's old age
was obviously an act of God. It showed God's
caring and power (Genesis 21:1-3).*

*God could have kept the three men from the fiery
furnace, but they would not have seen the power
and glory of God as they did (Daniel 3:19-27).*

IV. The important thing in adversity or suffering is not
    why, because the reason may never be known. More
    important is the way we react or respond to it. The
    fact is that God can be trusted. The question is, "Can
    He trust you?"

Share: *Do you respond with anger at your Creator: blaming, accusing, denying His goodness? Or, do you submit your will, determine to trust Him anyway, and allow the trial to help you grow in Him? In it all, do you recognize God's love?*

Read: Romans 8:28, 35-39

A. *We can trust God because His care is constant.* It is not sporadic, and it does not change with event or time. He has promised to be there at all times, and He is.

   Read: Genesis 28:15; Isaiah 43:1,2; 54:10; Hebrews 13:6

B. *We can trust God because His gifts are generous.* Twenty-six times the Psalmist declares that "His love endures forever" (Psalm 136). Love is the foundation of all His action. He generously spreads out the heavens, provides food for every creature, and does wondrous things for His people throughout the ages.

C. *God loves enough to bless, but also enough to withhold blessing or to allow adversity.* He knows that through adversity there will often be a greater understanding of Him. He knows the heart is deceitful and needs restraint if we are ever to be made into the image of the Creator.

   Read: Ephesians 2:10; Colossians 3:10

   Illustration:

A child who is indulged, given everything he wants, becomes demanding and selfish. Rather than being helped, he is hindered in life. He expects and demands immediate gratification. He is unwilling to submit to authority or to work for the fulfillment of his expectations.

V. Time may be needed for pruning, for growing, for learning, and for God to work in the lives of other people and situations; but, He can be trusted to work for the good of the one whose life is placed in His care. God is a loving Father who knows what it takes to teach His children to trust in Him. He is a great God; nothing is impossible or too hard for Him.

To Do at Home This Week: Lesson Five

1. God's promise to be with His people was given to several individuals or groups of people. Look up these promises. To whom was each one given and what did God say?

    Genesis 28:10-15_____

    _____

    Joshua 1:5_____

    _____

    Jeremiah 1:2,8_____

    _____

    Psalm 94:14_____

    _____

    Matthew 28:20_____

    _____

    Has God ever made this promise special to you? When? How did He keep His promise?

2. According to the NIV footnote on John 15:2, the word *prunes* also means *cleans* in the Greek.   In John 15:3 Jesus said, "You are already clean because of _____ _____."

From Ephesians 5:26,27, what is it that brings about the cleansing of the church, making her "without stain or wrinkle or any other blemish"?

_____

3. Find some scriptural reasons for adversity in the life of a believer:

1 Corinthians 11:29,30_____

_____

Hebrews 12:10,11_____

_____

James 1:2-4_____

_____

4. Share an example of some trial you have gone through that taught you something you may have never learned any other way.

Lesson Six

TALKING TO HIM

*"In everything, by prayer and petition, with thanksgiving,
present your requests to God." Philippians 4:6*

I. Review

    A. Ruth's response to the kindness of Boaz was one
of humility. She had courageously gone to work in
his fields, risking her status and personal safety.
Instead of becoming bitter and resentful, she
demonstrated thankfulness and willingly received
the help he offered her.

    B. It is not always easy to understand the reason for
adversity or loss, especially in the life of one who
is godly. Scripture gives many examples of those
who have been severely tested: Job, Joseph, Paul.

    C. The important thing in suffering is not why, but
how we react to it. We can learn and grow in
God, developing peace and righteousness. We can
develop more trust in Him, and we can learn to
empathize with others who suffer.

    D. One thing that helped Ruth make it through that
hot, difficult summer of gleaning was that she
stayed close..."close to the servant girls of Boaz."
Boaz was the source of her protection and
provision.

       Read: Ruth 2:21-23

II. God is our source of supply. Staying close to Him through the discipline of prayer brings the bountiful resources of heaven within reach.

Read: Psalm 42:1,2; 63:1; 143:6-8

A. Humankind was created with a spiritual dimension that the rest of God's creatures do not have: the ablility to understand, respond to, and trust in God. Other beings have physical bodies and some a psychological part, with intellect and personality and will. But only human beings have a spirit with the capacity and potential for full fellowship with their Creator.

Read: Romans 8:16; 1 Thessalonians 5:23

B. Understanding and accepting the love of God is key to effectual prayer. "...anyone who comes to Him must believe that He exists and that He rewards those who earnestly seek Him" (Hebrews 11:6).

Being convinced that it is God's desire to hear and to help brings confidence to trust Him in every situation. No need is too great or too small for the Heavenly Father's interest.

C. An awareness of God is cultivated in prayer. A rhythm of movement to and from God helps me know, "I am attached to God. I am loved by Him, cared for by Him, and guided by Him."

The goal of prayer should be to focus deliberately on Jesus, listen intently to His voice, and train our spirits to respond to Him.

Fellowship with God is available to all who will pursue it. Even at times when God's presence is not felt, there can be a confidence that He is there.

Read: Psalm 16:11; 145:18; Isaiah 55:6

III. Prayer is a learning process for the Christian, learned only in its practice. That is why the disciples asked the Lord, "Teach us *to* pray" - not "teach us *how* to pray," but rather teach us to *do* it! Regular prayer demands commitment: *a place, a time, and a plan.*

A. *The prayer place should be one where we can be alone with God.* The Bible calls it a "closet" and tells us we should "close the door" (Matthew 6:6). Distractions and interruptions make it difficult to enter into the presence of God.

Many find it is helpful to have a specific spot to which they return each time for prayer. A place where they are comfortable to pray quietly or aloud, to weep or to rejoice, or to alternate between reading the Word and praying. The place takes on a special aura when we regularly and freely converse with God there.

Illustration:
The patriarchs of old considered Bethel ("house of God") to be a place where God met them. Abraham (Genesis 12:8), Jacob (Genesis 28:11-

22), *Samuel (1 Samuel 7:15,16; 10:3), and Elisha (2 Kings 2:1-3) returned to Bethel for the express purpose of worshiping or meeting with God.*

When we are unable to return to our "Bethel," we can lift our voices to God wherever we are.

Read: Luke 18:1; Ephesians 6:18

B. *Prayer time should be adequate and unhurried.* It is more likely to be kept on a regular basis if observed at the same time each day.

Choose a time for prayer when the body is awake and alert. Walking or standing while praying helps a person stay awake. The "first business of the day" is a good motto, before business crowds the mind and obligations demand attention.

When living in a house with an unsaved mate or early-rising toddlers, the wee hours of the morning, lying quietly in bed, can be a rendezvous time with the Lord. Older children learn to respect a time of prayer if they see it is a priority to a parent.

The busier life becomes, the more desperately we need to take time to meet with God. Even the busiest person can make time for prayer once he realizes its importance. Jesus seems to have prayed long hours when the demands on Him were greatest. He also prayed short, on-the-spot prayers whenever and wherever He desired.

Read: Mark 1:35; Luke 6:12; 10:21; John 11:41

IV. *A prayer plan will help keep us from falling into the unbalanced prayer of "Give me, Lord."* A plan should include Scripture reading, meditation, Adoration, Confession, Thanksgiving, and intercession or Supplication: *ACTS.*

A. *Reading the Word of God helps open the door for communion with Him.* Meditating upon what it means and how it applies to one's life softens the heart for meaningful prayer. It is helpful to read each verse slowly until something arrests the attention, and then to stop and meditate before going on, considering its meaning and allowing it to nourish the spirit.

B. The order of a prayer plan will vary, but *worship (adoration)* is a good way to begin. The Psalmist said, "Enter his gates with thanksgiving and his courts with praise" (Psalm 100:4).

We *worship* Him because of *who He is.* We *praise* and thank Him for *what He has done.*

All worshiping people praise, but not all praising people worship. Some praise God as long as He is **doing** something for them, but when discouraged, they lose their reason to praise. Worship acknowledges God as almighty, full of mercy, love, and holiness, regardless of what is going on.

Read: 1 Chronicles 16:28,29; Psalm 95:6,7; John 4:23,24; Hebrews 13:15

C. *Confession.* Personal sin creates a barrier that can only be broken by repentance and confession. Reading the Scripture often leads to prayers of confession. It is impossible to pray effectively when the heart is heavy with conviction or guilt. A wrong relationship between husband and wife, or an unforgiving spirit toward others, can be a hindrance to prayer. God is always open to the prayer of repentance.

Read: Isaiah 59:1,2; Mark 11:25; 1 Peter 3:7,12

D. *Thanksgiving.* A thankful heart does away with discouragement and helps lift a spirit of depression. God requires that His people *praise* and *thank* Him. Thanksgiving helps us recognize how dependent we are on Him as the source of everything we need: food, clothing, shelter, emotional and physical health, salvation, and life itself.

Read: Ephesians 5:20; Philippians 4:6; 1 Timothy 2:1

Share: *What is going on in your life right now, today, for which you are thankful? Have you verbally expressed thanks to God and to the people who help you?*

E. *Supplication or Intercession (taking the place of another) is an important part of prayer.* Over and over Scripture instructs us to petition God for personal needs and to intercede for the needs of others. No need is too small, too great, too personal, or too difficult.

God has promised to meet all of our needs according to His glorious riches in Christ Jesus. Asking in Jesus' name means asking in cooperation with His will.

Read: Luke 11:9-13; John 14:13,14; Philippians 4:19; James 4:2,3

"Intercessory prayer," "praying through," and "a burden of prayer" - speak of travail as a woman giving birth. These terms indicate a wrestling, a fighting against powers that oppose the will of God. It is not wrestling with God to convince Him to answer, or to change His mind regarding a matter. It is praying to overcome the powers of darkness until God's people are brought to victory. The intercession of God's people can change the course of a nation.

Read: 2 Chronicles 7:14; Matthew 7:7,8; Ephesians 6:12,18

Illustration:
Daniel's prayer was heard the first day he prayed, but the answer was hindered for 21 days due to a prince of the kingdom of darkness. Daniel kept right on praying, bringing reinforcements from heaven (Daniel 10:12,13).

One way to intercede is to pray "in the Spirit." If we know how to pray, we pray with understanding.

If not, we can still pray effectively because the Spirit knows and prays through us.

Read: Romans 8:26,27; 1 Corinthians 14:14,15

F. Prayer is "the way we grope our way towards that which alone can satisfy our deepest need..."[8] In our need we come to God. Our loneliness, fear, rejection, and the problems of life are driving forces that bring us to Him.

Variety in the prayer time is the key to a consistent and successful prayer life. Change the method, the position, or the plan, but keep on praying.

---

[8]Maxie Dunnam, *The Workbook on Spiritual Disciplines* (Nashville, TN: The Upper Room), p. 42.

Finding God in the Tangles of Life

To Do at Home This Week: Lesson Six

1. What specific things are we instructed to pray for in
    the following scriptures?

    Psalm 2:8

    _____

    Psalm 122:6

    _____

    Matthew 5:44

    _____

    Luke 10:2

    _____

    Luke 22:40

    _____

    1 Timothy 2:1-4

    _____

2. James 5:13-16 gives instruction concerning prayer. Can you identify the various kinds of prayer referred to in these verses?

petition_____

praise_____

intercession_____

confession_____

3. Do you ever feel your prayers are being hindered by something? Examine your own life and heart as to what the cause may be as you look up the following verses:

Psalm 66:18_____

Ezekiel 14:3_____

Mark 11:25_____

James 1:5-7_____

James 4:3_____

1 Peter 3:7_____

Lesson Seven

HEARING FROM HIM

"Your ears will hear a voice behind you, saying, 'This is the way; walk in it.'" Isaiah 30:21

I. Review

    A. God created mankind with a spiritual dimension the rest of creation does not have: a spirit that can respond, understand, and trust in God. We cultivate an awareness of God as we pray.

    B. The battle for a life of consistent prayer is never over. We struggle to establish a place, a time, and a plan for ongoing, faithful prayer times.

    C. A prayer plan should include: reading the Word of God, meditating on Him and on His Word, adoring, confessing, and thanking, as well as interceding for needs.

II. In chapter 3 of *Ruth* we see Naomi forming a plan that will serve to answer the prayer she prayed in Ruth 1:8,9. The grain harvest was coming to a close, winter would soon arrive, and the future was still uncertain.

Read: Ruth 3:1-4

    A. Naomi was concerned for the future of her much-loved daughter-in-law. She recognized the providence of God in leading Ruth to the fields of Boaz. Since he had shown such kindness to Ruth and was a kinsman (a near relative), Boaz was the logical one to turn to for help.

B. Old Testament law provided that if a family was forced to mortgage property due to poverty, and was then unable to make the payments, a blood relative could go to civil court and redeem him and his property. This individual was called a kinsman-redeemer.

If the original owner died without an heir, it became the duty of the kinsman-redeemer to marry his widow and raise up children in the name of the deceased. A redeemer must be both *willing* and *able* to redeem: *willing* to assume responsibility for their care, and *able* to pay the price for purchase of the property.

Read: Leviticus 25:47-55

C. Redemption includes the idea of paying a price, not just setting a slave free or delivering him from a slave owner.

Redemption is never cheap. Yahweh redeemed His people from the yoke of the Egyptians with great effort and cost to himself. Jesus bought men at the price of His own blood, becoming a "ransom for many."

Read: Exodus 6:6; Mark 10:45; 1 Corinthians 6:20

III. Courtship customs differ greatly from culture to culture. Ruth's coming to the threshing floor in the middle of the night reflects the urgency she and Naomi felt about their plight. They must present their legal rights to Boaz.

Naomi's plan included Ruth's going to the threshing floor where Boaz would be winnowing barley. Her action was daring and risky: what if he refused? What if he took advantage of her vulnerability in the night? What if someone saw her and interpreted her presence as that of a prostitute, thereby threatening her chances for a legitimate redemption?

A. The threshing floor was a large open space of exposed bedrock or hard, stamped earth. The grain was first bundled in the field, then carried by hand, beast, or cart to the threshing floor. There it was beaten with a toothed sledge, trampled under animal hooves (Micah 4:13), or crushed under cart wheels (Isaiah 28:28), to remove the husks from the kernels.

With a fork or shovel, the mixture was then tossed into the air where the wind carried the lighter chaff and dust away. The straw blew to the side and the grain (which was heaviest) fell to the floor. Usually this was done in the evening when the wind was blowing gently. The kernels of grain were collected in piles and the straw fed as fodder to animals.

Illustration: Luke 22:31
Jesus used the analogy of the harvest when He told Peter of Satan's desire to sift him "as wheat." The metaphor of sifting implies separating what is desirable from what is undesirable.

B. Naomi knew Boaz would remain at the threshing floor for the night, perhaps to protect the readied grain from robbers, but also to be a part of the festivities.

She instructed Ruth to prepare herself for this encounter (3:3). She was to take a bath, dress up in her finest, and put on some perfume. She was to go where Boaz was, at a time when he would be happy, contented, and not distracted by the presence of others or by work demands.

Naomi set up the most favorable situation possible. She chose a place where the couple could talk completely alone for the first time. However, Ruth was not to initiate the conversation but to watch very carefully where he laid down and then go and lay down quietly at his feet. A man of his stature would be turned off by aggressiveness on her part.

In the middle of the night Boaz was startled to find a woman lying at his feet - a place where servants often lay. In the darkness he could not tell who she was.

C. Her request, "Spread the corner of your garment over me, since you are a kinsman-redeemer" (3:9), was a request for commitment. A marriage proposal if you will.

The Hebrew word for *uncovering* of his feet occurs primarily in expressions describing a variety of illicit sexual relations. The threshing floor was popularly associated with licentiousness.[9]

The expression "uncovering the feet" is also used by God to describe what He did for Israel when He made a commitment to care for her.

Read: Ezekiel 16:8-13; Hosea 9:1

Ruth was humbly, desperately requesting his protection even at the risk of being considered sexually suggestive. She had now done all she could. She had stated her need, asked for his help, and made herself available.

D. Boaz responded with reassurance, tenderness, and a promise. He promised to be Ruth's *goel,* or "kinsman-redeemer," if a nearer kin would not redeem her. He demonstrated his righteousness by determining to settle things through proper means and leave the outcome to God. She was not to worry but to lie down and sleep for the rest of the night.

IV. Ruth's experience at the threshing floor provides a great lesson in coming to God. She presented her need, received his promise, and waited in trust for the answer. God has promised to lead those who trust Him and are willing to obey. In order that we might be sure

---

[9]Robert L. Hubbard, Jr. *The New International Commentary on the Old Testament the Book of Ruth,* p.203.

we are hearing from God, He has provided several ways of communicating His answer to us.

A. *God speaks through the conscience.* Much of the Holy Spirit's guidance comes from Him without our being aware of it. He gives wisdom or a quiet confidence in situations that could otherwise be upsetting or confusing. He often warns of danger, cautions in temptation, or reveals future plans to the listening heart.

Read: John 16:13: 1 Corinthians 6:19; Isaiah 30:21

Because a person's own voice, desires, and thoughts also speak, other means of guidance are needed to be sure that what is heard is from the Lord.

B. *God's guidance will always line up with His written Word, which is the final judge.* The Word always upholds righteousness, purity, fairness, and honesty.

The Bible is a fascinating chronicle of how God led men and women through the ages. Their experiences are written down as examples and warnings (1 Corinthians 10:11). The Bible is a basic primer on techniques of working with people, living in a marriage, or running a business. We can trust the Word to communicate God's message to us as we acquaint ourselves with it.

When read regularly, God's Word will renew the mind and get deep inside the spirit until it abides

Finding God in the Tangles of Life

within and creates an armor against the enemy -a belt of truth around the waist (Ephesians 6:14).

Read: Psalm 119:105; Isaiah 2:3; Hebrews 4:12

C. *God guides by the circumstances of life.* He opens and closes doors of opportunity to reveal His will. Circumstances work for us when we are on the right track. There is no need to shove, push, run over people, or sin. God will make a way, just as He did for the nation of Israel and for Ruth, as a person moves in His will.

Read: Jeremiah 32:21; Revelation 3:7,8

Share: Why do you think it was important that Boaz allow the judicial system of his day to clear the way for marriage to Ruth?

D. *God uses the wise counsel of friends, godly leaders, and teachers who help us understand the principles of the Word or who apply wisdom and common sense in an objective way.* Counselors should be godly people, committed to being followers of His Word.

Read: Proverbs 12:15; 15:22; Ephesians 4:11,12

E. *Sometimes God confirms what He is saying by a word of wisdom, a prophecy, a dream, a vision, or some other supernatural demonstration.*

Read: Acts 5:1-10; 10:9-20; 16:9,10

It is necessary that all of the above points agree with each other if we are to truly know God's will in a matter. Not any one of them should be taken as guidance by itself.

V. Too many times we struggle to know God's will. It will be found more quickly when the duties and challenges of the day are accepted as His will for now.

"To learn God's will, take your gifts, buckle down, and use your talents in the local church as if you plan to stay there all your life. God will move you if He wants, when He wants." (Evangelist Joe Arnett)[10]

A. In the pre-dawn darkness as Ruth got up to leave, Boaz filled her shawl with a generous portion of grain. It was something she had not asked for. Something that would relieve the worry of food for the winter ahead.

B. As we seek the Lord and wait for His guidance, we learn to recognize His voice. We do not demand of God but trust Him to lead and guide our footsteps. Perfect trust teaches that it is not only God's will to hear a prayer, but to give the best and richest answer He can.

Read: Psalm 4:3; 37:23,24; John 10:3-5

---

[10]Joyce Landorf, *The High Cost of Growing* (New York, NY: Thomas Nelson, Inc., 1978), p.110.

Finding God in the Tangles of Life

To Do at Home This Week: Lesson Seven

1. Read chapter 3 of *Ruth* again and take note of the following:

   What characteristics did Ruth portray in going to Boaz at the threshing floor?

   Why do you think Naomi urged her to go?

2. Why is it essential for Christians to study God's Word:

   John 8:31,32_____

   _____

3. Review again the ways God leads us by looking up the following Scriptures:

   Psalm 119:105_____

   John 16:13,14_____

   Acts 2:17,18_____

   Ephesians 4:11,12_____

Revelation 3:8_____

4. Guidance can be received from God as we pray. What happened in each of the following instances as a direct answer to prayer?

Acts 10:1-7

1 Kings 3:10-15

Acts 12:1-17

5. During your prayer times this week, take special care to spend at least a few minutes quietly listening to the Holy Spirit. Be sure your mind has been prepared to receive by reading the Word first. Are you hearing anything special from God for your life?

Lesson Eight

WAITING FOR HIM

"It is good to wait quietly for the salvation of the Lord."
Lamentations 3:26

I. Review

    A. From Ruth's experience with Boaz at the threshing floor, we learn we must present our needs to God. He wants us to ask, to give Him access to the situation, and then wait for Him to act.

    B. When we come to Him in prayer, He gives us His promise that He will not only hear us but will answer: "Ask whatever you will and it shall be done unto you" (John 15:7). Sometimes we receive that for which we did not ask, or an answer that is different from what we expected.

    C. God has promised to give guidance to His children and does so in several ways: through the conscience, through His written Word, through the circumstances of life, the wise counsel of friends, and sometimes by a supernatural demonstration (dream, vision, prophecy, etc.).

        All must line up together if we are to be sure of His leading. Timing is just as important as the method of guidance.

II. Ruth had done all she could to present her need to Boaz. She had made herself available to be his wife. Now all she could do was wait.

Read: Ruth 3:7-18

Waiting is perhaps the most difficult thing you and I do, especially in a country where we live by the clock and run our lives at a frenzied pace.

A. We all know about waiting in doctors' offices, restaurant lines, at stoplights or in motor vehicle service stations. We wait for news from a loved one, for a business deal to be consummated, for special events to arrive, and sometimes several years for a new home or a special vacation.

But we don't like it. We are programmed to see results. We want answers. We are told, "Get it now. Don't wait!" We provide credit cards, fax machines, and car phones to hurry the process.

B. God seems to use the waiting process to force us into a position of dependency and trust. He knows that in the waiting times we will need to put our trust in Him. When there is no instant answer, we turn to the One who is ultimately in charge of all things.

Sometimes we wait for God to answer an earnest prayer for healing, or for help in a relationship. At times it seems like financial relief, or wisdom in a situation is a long time in coming.

C. Scripture is full of waiters. David said, "I am worn out calling for help; my throat is parched. "My eyes fail, looking for my God" ("while I wait for my God"-KJV) (Psalm 69:3).

-Noah waited 120 years before it rained.

-Job waited possibly 60-70 years for his help and restoration.

-Abraham waited 100 years to receive the promise of a son and never did find the city he sought.

-Joseph waited in prison for 14 years on false charges before he was remembered and released.

-Moses lived as a shepherd in the desert for 40 years before God finally called him and made him leader of the Israelites.

-Over and over the Psalmist talks about being still and waiting on the Lord.

-Our friends, Ruth and Naomi, waited a good while before seeing their dream of a happy life fulfilled.

Read: Psalm 37:7,9; Isaiah 8:17; 40:31

Illustration: Habakkuk 1-3
One who purposefully waited on the Lord was Habakkuk. Chapter 1 reveals his frustration at the sin and injustice of the world. He feels God is not listening and the wicked are winning over the righteous.

In chapter 2 he decides there are no other options than to wait and see what God will answer. Will God let them get away with their sin?

God's response was that the answer will come at the appointed time. It will be true and fair. In essence, God told Habakkuk, "Be patient and wait for I wait with you. You are not alone!"

Chapter 3 brings Habakkuk's conclusion that no matter what happens, whether he sees an answer or not, whether he understands or not, he will trust in God (3:17-19).

III. Good things happen when we wait.

A. *We learn to appreciate the everyday things: people, pleasures, routines, and work.*

Most of life is made up of the mundane things....the necessities for existence. The maintenance of home, family, body, and possessions brings a sense of belonging. Work that needs to be done and demands concentration and strength, brings a feeling of contentment.

Quiet, ordinary, boring days cause a person to sit back and observe the Lord's workings. Confidence and trust are learned as He is allowed to demonstrate His love throughout a normal day.

Exciting events or miracles happen only occasionally in anyone's life. Whether at home, at work, or in the spiritual life, who could stand the strain of trauma, or party, or miracle, every minute?

Read: Ecclesiastes 5:18-20

B. *We are able to see God's long-term plan more clearly as time goes by.* Instant answers may get in the way of what He wants to do. Insisting on immediate answers may cause us to miss the greater miracle that God desires for us.

Illustrations:
Joseph probably prayed for deliverance when his brothers threw him into the well and then sold him to traders from Egypt. What if God had answered (Genesis 37:1-36; 45:8; 50:20)?

The Israelites demanded meat and got it, but they lost the sweetness of God's presence (Exodus 16:11,12; Psalm 106:15).

Many faithful servants of the Lord never saw what they had hoped for. Why? "These were all commended for their faith, yet none of them received what had been promised. God had planned something better for us so that only together with us would they be made perfect" (Hebrews 11:39,40).

C. *Changes take place as we wait.* We mature. We grow. Attitudes and subsequently demands are changed. God is able to work in the hearts of others involved, and to bring about changes that are necessary for the fulfillment of His will.

Read: Lamentations 3:25,26

D. *We get to know God more personally as we wait.* It is important to wait in silence, not run to other people telling our woes, but to "be still and know God." He is sovereign and able to see us through every situation.

Read: Psalm 46:10

IV. Today Christians wait expectantly for the return of the Lord Jesus. This is the hope of the Christian--the promise that keeps him going. Called the "blessed hope," it is the anticipation of His coming that makes waiting worthwhile.

   A. The Early Church believed that the Lord would return at any moment.

   Read: 1 Corinthians 7:29-31; 1 Thessalonians 4:13-18; Titus 2:13.

   B. The doctrine of the second coming of Jesus is referred to more than 300 times in the New Testament (one verse in every 13) and in Paul's epistles at least 50 times.

   Whole chapters (Matthew 24, Mark 13) and whole books (1 & 2 Thessalonians), are given to the subject of the Lord's coming.

   C. Our hope is not in death, nor in the prospect of converting the world, but in the appearance of the Bridegroom. Apart from Him there is no meaning to life with all its problems.

   Read: Colossians 3:1-4

D. Jesus will once more invade the world order, this time to set things right. His coming is an incentive for holy living. Its hope stimulates Christian service and helps us reevaluate the priorities that govern our standard of living. Hope inspires endurance when life is difficult.

Read: Matthew 24:44; 2 Corinthians 5:10; 1 Thessalonians 1:3; 1 Peter 1:8; 1 John 2:28

E. The coming of Jesus is portrayed in Scripture as the time when He will receive His own to be with Him forever.

He will return *personally*: John 14:3

He will return *unexpectedly*: Matthew 24:36,42; Mark 13:35

He will return *physically*: Acts 1:11 - this *same* Jesus.

Read: 1 Thessalonians 4:16,17

V. Our purpose in this life is much higher than the pursuit of pleasure, or riches, or good health. So soon, these are gone. Even fame or a good name are often short-lived. We are created for the glory of our Maker.

Read: Isaiah 43:7; Revelation 4:11

A. We find reason for living when we fulfill God's purpose for us.

Though we are rejected, discouraged, or bruised by the hurts of life, we wait for our renewal to come. "The whole creation has been groaning, as in the pains of childbirth right up to the present time....we groan inwardly as we *wait eagerly* for our adoption as sons, the redemption of our bodies" (Romans 8:22, 23).

B. Little did Ruth know the far-reaching effects of her decisions: to move to Bethlehem, to glean in the fields of Boaz, to faithfully serve and support and love her mother-in-law, and to work and wait all through the harvest and heat of the summer. It was all very mundane, wearying, even boring, but it paved the way for the greatest event in history - the coming of the Messiah.

Share: Are you waiting for something important in your life right now? What is your attitude toward this period of seeming delay? What, if anything, have you learned in the process?

To Do at Home This Week: Lesson Eight

1. Can you find any good reason for Ruth to wait several months before Boaz could be approached as her kinsman-redeemer?

   How important is timing in pursuing our "rights"?

2. Ruth, a heathen Moabite, became part of the lineage of the Messiah and Redeemer. Trace the lineage of Jesus in Matthew 1. Who are the other women mentioned in the genealogy?

3. Compare the law regarding the Moabite in Nehemiah 13:1-3 with what God did for Ruth. Why do you think He did this?

4. What is the most difficult wait you have experienced in your life? Are you in a waiting period now? What comfort do you find in the following scriptures?

Isaiah 3:10_____

Isaiah 40:31_____

1 John 3:2,3_____

4. Ruth's rewards were earthly as well as spiritual. List some of the eternal rewards promised to the faithful Christian as found in the following scriptures:

1 Corinthians 9:24,25_____

2 Timothy 4:7,8_____

James 1:12_____

Revelation 2:7_____

Revelation 22:4,5_____

Lesson Nine

LIVING FOR HIM

"You will keep in perfect peace him whose mind is steadfast, because he trusts in you." Isaiah 26:3

I. Review

   A. Waiting on the Lord to work in our lives brings about some good things: more dependency and trust in Him, greater appreciation for the everyday things, realization of the long-range plan of God, and the changing of our desires and attitudes.

   B. The hope of the Christian is the return of the Lord Jesus. We wait for that day with great expectation and excitement for He will return in the same manner as He left: personally, physically, and unexpectedly. This hope helps keep us faithful when life is mundane or difficult.

II. When Boaz left the threshing floor after his meeting with Ruth, he went immediately to the "town gate and sat there" (4:1). He did not delay or renege on his promise to Ruth.

Read: Ruth 4:1-12

   A. The town gate was the best place to locate other near kinsman. Everyone had to pass through the gate to go to the fields, the threshing floor, or to other cities.

      Ancient cities were built very compactly along narrow streets, but the gate area provided a public place spacious enough for people to congregate. Usually there was a large area in front of the wall's outer edge, and another spacious, bench-lined open area just inside it.

Like a modern town square or plaza, the gate area was both marketplace and news center for the community. The gate was the place where legal transactions took place. It was the courthouse where officials sat to administer justice and to oversee legal transactions. Prophets addressed kings there and the heathen often used the open area for a place to offer sacrifices to their gods.

Read: 1 Kings 22:10; 2 Kings 23:8; Nehemiah 8:1,3; Jeremiah 17:19-25; Acts 14:13

B. The gate was a busy place in the morning "rush hour," and it was no problem for Boaz to obtain elders and witnesses for the legal transaction of property rights.

When the near kinsman arrived, Boaz requested him to sit down. Boaz wanted this transaction to be legal and valid. The onlookers gathered about to hear what was happening.

C. Boaz's determination to be Ruth's kinsman-redeemer in a legal fashion, and with the blessing of the elders, reflected his desire to establish a home in peace, to begin the marriage union with blessing rather than opposition and criticism.

III. Peace is the number one thing desired by the young, the old, and everyone in between. Peace at home, on the job, and in the world. How often it eludes us and how we strive for it in our lives!

Illustration:
A doctor in Oklahoma City asked his patients over many years, "If you had an Aladdin's lamp and could have anything you wished for, what would it be?" All but three said the same thing: "Peace, inner peace."

A. The Hebrew word for peace *shalom* is found 250 times in the Old Testament. Its meaning signifies "wholeness." It speaks of being finished, made perfect and complete. Both Old and New Testaments use the word as a greeting.

B. The commonly accepted meaning of peace is "freedom from strife." However, peace has more to do with what is going on inside a person than with external things. Peace involves serenity beyond the facade - a freedom from worry, mental turmoil, despair, and frustration. It speaks of a confidence and inward happiness, not related to outward beauty or circumstances.

C. Peace with God is the beginning place. When we go away from the God who made us, we are left with an insatiable restlessness within. No amount of success, material blessing, or number of relationships can fill the void.

Read: Isaiah 53:5; 57:20-21; Romans 3:17

D. It takes effort to live in peace (Romans 14:19). Even for the Christian, peace is not automatic but must be pursued. A peaceful home or contented life does not come about by accident or chance. Peaceful living requires proper choices, planning, and effort.

Outside pressures of temptation, business, and difficult relationships, as well as the sinful nature within all of us, cause stress and challenge a peaceful existence.

Illustrations:
David, popular, beloved King of Israel, apple of God's eye, found himself fleeing from Saul and later from his own offspring, battling starvation, and living as a fugitive. It was he who penned the words, "Seek peace and pursue it" (Psalm 34:14).

Jeremiah, the prophet who ministered to the Jews taken captive to Babylon, told them to "seek the peace and prosperity of the city" to which they had been taken (Jeremiah 29:7).

E. We are not asking or expecting that all stress be removed from life. Some pressure is necessary to help us grow physically, emotionally, spiritually and mentally. Single, married, with or without family - all know stress. Every stage of life has its own pressures that we try in vain to escape.

Share: *What are some stress points in your life? Are they normal for your age group?*

F. Life will often bring unexpected stress, sudden things we have no control over: death, sickness, financial loss. Unless we have stored up a reserve of peace-producing habits, we may find ourselves crushed under the weight of stress. Even small disappointments can be too much for the one whose life is without inner peace.

Illustration:
In April 1963, the nuclear submarine Thresher *vanished about 200 miles off the coast of New England. It had been undergoing deep submergence tests when radio contact was lost. It had gone deeper than it was pressurized to go, and in one terrifying moment the greater pressure outside the sub brought the ocean in like jets of steam. One-hundred, twenty-nine American sailors were lost. The outside pressure was more than the* Thresher *was prepared to handle.*

IV. Jesus desires to give us His peace through the work of the Holy Spirit.

Read: John 14:27; Galatians 5:22

However, there are destructive forces at work to eliminate peace. The whole world is crying "Peace, peace...when there is no peace" (Jeremiah 6:14). Why is it that so few ever experience real peace?

A. *Peace is destroyed by always wanting more....*more possessions, more from people, more success, more recognition. Comparison is where discontent begins. Learning to be content and thankful for what we have, where we are, and who we are helps bring peace.

Read: Romans 8:5,6; 1 Timothy 6:6-8

B. *Peace is destroyed by unforgiveness....*allowing a bitter root to grow. A person is not free to fully know joy and peace as long as there is bondage to the hurts of the past. Animosity, hostility, jealousy, and bitterness produce problems, not peace. Whatever has been suffered: verbal or physical abuse, unfair treatment, or disappointments of any kind, all must be forgiven and put in the past without thought of revenge.

Read: Luke 6:27,28; 1 Thessalonians 5:13; Hebrews 12:15

C. *Peace is destroyed by refusing to give up a pet sin.* Rebellion against our Maker and the laws He has given will result in guilt, confusion, and unhappiness. Submission to God's will and way is a sure path to peace. Secret sin may never be found out by those closest to us, but harboring it in the heart and mind will affect all we do.

Read: Psalm 38:4-8; Isaiah 48:18; Romans 6:11-13; James 3:18

D. *Peace is destroyed by allowing small things to accumulate or control daily living.* There is little peace to be found in a messy, disorganized, or dirty house: laundry undone or not folded and put away, drawers and closets full to overflowing, dirty dishes left to harden in the sink, and magazines and mail cluttering every table and chair. The effort it takes to keep things in place pays off with the resulting peace.

Read: Proverbs 31:27; Song of Solomon 2:15; Romans 14:19

E. *Peace is destroyed when time is wasted:* too much TV, too much time spent on hobbies, sports, physical fitness, plants, pets, magazines, or telephone. Good things...but when allowed to control, they bring tension to the home.

Read: 1 Corinthians 6:12

F. *Cluttering the calendar with too many obligations or forgotten commitments disturbs the peace.* Learning to set priorities, and to say no to unnecessary demands of people, can help bring peace.

Read: Psalm 90:12

G. *A high noise level in a house can affect its peace.* Communication that is gentle and nonargumentive, and children who are well disciplined (trained), contribute to an atmosphere where peace can reign. Music can help or hinder. Table covers can reduce clatter. Rugs can soften footsteps. When adults use soft voices and refrain from calling to each other from one end of the house to the other, it is easier to control the noise level of small children.

Read: Proverbs 15:1; 29:17; Isaiah 32:18

V. Peace is the result of practicing peace-producing habits on a regular, ongoing basis. Making them a part of daily living assures us that we will not be overwhelmed by the unexpected pressures life may bring.

   A. *Make a commitment to live in peace with the people whose lives you share.* Time is needed to listen to each other, pray together, plan together, and work at tasks together. A family should eat together as often as possible, and help one another when the pressure is on. Family and friends are needed in times of joy and sorrow. When trusting relationships are built, a harbor is provided from the inevitable storms of life.

   Read: Matthew 5:9; Ephesians 4:32; 5:19; 6:1-4

   B. *Guard carefully the times God has designed for rest and recovery.* No matter how busy or how demanding a schedule is, God has said, "...even during the plowing season and harvest you must rest" (Exodus 34:21). He planned it that way.

   Burnout is a new word. *Stress* was once used to describe the weight or pressure a building could take before it would collapse. The word now applies to people. Two-thirds of family doctor visits are prompted by stress-related symptoms. Insomnia, heart disease, cancer, lung ailments, and suicide are being related more and more to the patterns of a stressful life.

The American Institute of Stress participated in more than 200 stress-related studies over a three-year period. Magazines, newspapers, and TV reports compile information to help American adults deal with the disease of the day - stress. At the top of their list of advice is relaxation.

It takes planning and discipline to take advantage of the rest times God has provided: a special day of the week set aside for worship and communication with God, a nighttime of darkness conducive to sleep, and special holidays designed for joyous celebration with family and friends. Observed, these times bring release from stress. Ignored, pressures build and the body breaks.

Read: Genesis 2:2; Psalm 4:8; Isaiah 30:29

C. *Keep a quiet time with God.* A daily time of communion with the Creator brings His peace-giving presence. It helps us sort out the unimportant and concentrate on the eternal. Allowing our thoughts to return to Him often, and to remember the Holy Word that we have stored up in our hearts, will help us find peace in the midst of the most hectic day.

Read: Isaiah 26:3; 30:15

VI. Only the God who made us is able to still the storm within and bring peace. Jesus alone can bring us peace because He purchased it with His life. Peace with God and with mankind, in the midst of a world of conflict, is the true "shalom."

9-Living for Him   97

To Do at Home This Week: Lesson Nine

1. From the following scriptures discover ways of living that will help bring peace into your life:

   Isaiah 26:3_____

   Exodus 34:21_____

   Ephesians 4:26,27_____

   Deuteronomy 11:1,19,20_____

2. According to scripture, peace is not passive or automatic. It takes_____ (Romans 14:19) and we must _____it (Psalm 34:14).

3. What would you consider to be stress points at the following stages of life?

   for a child:_____

   for a teenager:_____

   for a young adult:_____

   for a middle-aged person:_____

   for a senior adult:_____

Are the pressures you face every day within the normal range for your age group? Do you see some way to relieve some of the stress from your life? How?

4. Is there something or someone in your life who keeps tearing down your peace? What did Paul say he did with past hurts and failures? (Philippians 3:13,14)

5. First Corinthians 14:33 says, "God is not a God of disorder but of peace." The author is referring to church involvement, but since God is always the same and has the same standards for home and church, how could you apply this to a household or to a family?

Lesson Ten

FAILING HIM

"If anybody does sin, we have one who speaks to the Father in our defense—Jesus Christ, the Righteous One."
1 John 2:1

I. Review

   A. Naomi returned to Bethlehem after 10 years in Moab, an idolatrous country which God himself had said would be cursed (Isaiah 15). She came humbly, needy, willing to work and to wait for God's help.

   Ruth came to Boaz asking him for mercy and for the covering of his mantle.

   B. In the story of Ruth we see a beautiful symmetry of what Jesus does for us: Boaz is a graphic type of Christ Jesus who is kind, merciful, and able to help us. Ruth signifies the believer who comes in need and receives His mercy; Orpah, who returned to Moab, is a type of the unbeliever who returns to the gods of this world. Naomi appears as the wise counselor, much like the Holy Spirit, who gives direction and gently urges us toward the Lord.

   C. The circumstances were not perfect. Ruth was a Moabitess, not an Israelite. She had to take the part of a lowly servant. She knew persecution and rejection. With a potentially negative future, Ruth was thrust into a position of acceptance, love, and promise.

II. Righteousness in the sight of God is based not on our performance, but on our faith in God who is our righteousness.

Ruth was blessed because she chose to follow the ways of Abraham and of God's people, not because of her bloodline. Yet she became the great-grandmother of King David in the lineage of Christ.

The wedding wish given to Ruth and Boaz, "May the Lord make the woman who is coming into your home like Rachel and Leah," declared God's blessing in spite of a less-than-perfect heritage.

Read: Ruth 4:9-12

A. The Israelites' history was one of failure, disobedience, and sordid sin. Yet it pleased God to bring order out of chaos.

Illustration: Genesis 29:16-30
Both Rachel and Leah had a place in history even though they were married to Jacob with deceit and lies on the part of their father. They were blessed with children who became part of the ancestral line of Christ Jesus.

B. At first glance, Scriptures seem to promise good for those who are perfect and punishment for those who fail.

Read: Psalm 24:3,4; 119:1-3; 1 John 3:8,9

The fact is that both those described as *evil* and those described as *righteous* are basically sinful. In themselves, they fail at being pure or righteous. God's blessing is promised to the one whose deep desire is to listen, follow, and obey - not to the one who is perfectly without sin or failure.

The difference is in the attitude of the heart. The "pure in heart" delight in God's words (law) and in His presence. They acknowledge Him in all their ways. They hate evil, are grieved by their own failure, and see themselves as needing God.

The one described in Scripture as *evil,* desires to go his own way without God. He loves darkness, enjoys the company of the wicked, and participates in sinful acts.

Read: Isaiah 1:18-20; Romans 3:20,23; 4:3; 2 Peter 1:3

Illustration:
Even the most devoted follower of the Lord fails at times. Abraham, Moses, and David, looked to as examples of faith, each had times of failure. All kept coming back to God with repentant hearts each time they experienced the overwhelming influence of evil.

C. We come to God from where we are, with all our past failures, weaknesses, and sin. He always receives the penitent heart. He brings good out of failure for the one who repents.

Read: Romans 3:22; 10:4; 1 Corinthians 1:30; Ephesians 2:8,9

D. God describes His children as sheep, dumb animals, prone to wander, and oblivious to enemies; not as foxes, wily and clever. Therefore He makes it simple for us: "Obey Me, but be sorry when you don't." Confess your sin and get back on track.

Read: Isaiah 53:6; John 10:27; 1 John 1:10

Share: *Has there been a time in your life when you felt you failed God? Was it deliberate? What do you think caused the failure? How did God respond? How did the church respond?*

III. When we fail again and again, we may feel we will never know victory in this Christian life. When Christians fail to listen, follow, or obey Him, what is God's response?

A. *HE DOES NOT: Condemn.* He does not say, "You are no good; you'll never make it." He knows the requirements for righteousness are possible only in Jesus.

Read: Romans 8:1,2

B. *HE DOES NOT: Condone or excuse sin.* He does not say, "That's OK, I know you are weak, and I understand you must sin a little." He does not remove all consequences of disobedience.

Read: Galatians 6:7,8

C. *HE DOES NOT: Take away free choice.* He leaves both bad and good options open to us. The choice of which road we will follow is ours. Serving God is a daily decision to choose His way.

Read: Deuteronomy 30:15-18; Joshua 24:15; Proverbs 1:29-31

D. When we fail, *GOD DOES: Convict.* A person's conscience will bear witness of right or wrong. The Holy Spirit within will prod, "This is the way." We can be thankful for the uncomfortable prodding of the conscience that keeps us aware of wrong.

Read: Romans 2:15; 2 Corinthians 1:12

E. *HE DOES: Put up roadblocks* - warnings to keep us from going the wrong direction. These may come to us through Scripture reading, sermons, advice of people, or circumstances. Recognizing the authorities God has placed in our lives helps us keep on track.

Read: Isaiah 30:21; Zechariah 7:12; Romans 13:1,2; Hebrews 1:1,2

F. *HE DOES: Forgive.* God always accepts and cleanses the repentant heart. He blots out the past and holds none of our failure or sin against us.

Read: 2 Chronicles 7:14; Psalm 51:12; 103:12;
1 John 1:9

IV. We have a gracious Heavenly Father who has made provision for us to live in victory. He does not want us to be overcome with failure. He has provided everything we need for living a victorious Christian life.

Read: 2 Peter 1:3

A. *God has provided the Holy Spirit who lives within us.* He is our Comforter (John 14:16, 26), our Teacher (John 16:13), the One who convicts us of sin (John 16:8) and reveals Jesus to us (John 16:14; Ephesians 1:17). He helps us pray (Romans 8:26) and gives us strength to live through faith (Ephesians 3:16).

The Holy Spirit is the seal of Christ's promise: a deposit guaranteeing our inheritance.

Read: 2 Corinthians 1:22; 5:5; Ephesians 1:14

Without the Holy Spirit, the things of God cannot be discerned. He teaches us the doctrines and the do's and don'ts of acceptable behavior. He turns on the light so we see our sin. Because of spiritual blindness, we may fail to see our own unforgiving spirit, unfairness, harshness, ungrateful attitude, selfishness, or unyielding ways.

The Spirit reveals these to us, not to bring us to despair, but to repentance. As the Holy Spirit reveals our shortcomings in comparison to the holiness of God, He creates a desire in us to be like Him. We want to please the Father. Day-by-day He gives us strength to live above the carnal nature and in obedience to God.

Read: 1 Corinthians 2:14; 2 Corinthians 7:10; 2 Timothy 1:14

B. *God has given us the Holy Scriptures to show us how to live and what the result of disobedience will be.* They assure us that God is near and will never fail us.

Reading the Word of God builds our faith by bringing hope through the precious promises found therein. We respond to the examples set by godly men and women who have gone before us.

Read: Psalm 119:11,105, 130

C. *God provides the church and its assigned pastors, teachers, prophets, and evangelists to teach us.* They help us grow in our spiritual walk, and bring us to repentance and restoration when we falter.

We can strengthen the ministry of the church in the community by making a commitment to be faithful in attendance, in giving, and in the support of church programs and leaders.

As we seek to minister and serve within the local body, the gifts function and we grow in grace. It is here that we learn to forgive and to love.

Read: Ephesians 4:11-13

D. *God also gives us the watchful care of angels who are His messengers,* "sent to serve those who will inherit salvation" (Hebrews 1:14). Who knows how many times these mighty warriors intervene when Satan would destroy us?

E. As if all of these provisions were not enough, *the Lord Jesus himself is interceding for us before the Heavenly Father.* He wants us to succeed in our Christian walk.

Read: Hebrews 7:25; 1 John 2:1

V. The lessons Ruth learned as a gleaner were invaluable to her as head of her husband's estate. Those months in the field prepared her for ruling with him and sharing in a kingdom which had been strange to her.

God wants us to live above failure and in victory, but more than that, He wants us to learn obedience. He wants us to learn principles of the Kingdom, how they work, and how we can tap into their benefits.

To Do at Home This Week: Lesson Ten

1. Review *Ruth* chapters 2, 3, and 4.

   List as many positive character qualities of Boaz as you can find:

   What quality do you appreciate most about him?

2. Jesus is our example of holiness. Identify some of these characteristics in the following Scriptures. Have you experienced these qualities in your own life?

   Matthew 27:13,14:_____

   Mark 10:45   _____

   Luke 23:34   _____

   John 13:1; 15:13_____

3. Contrast "walking in the Spirit" and "walking in the flesh," according to Galatians 5:16-25. List the characteristics of each:

WALKING IN THE SPIRIT:

WALKING IN THE FLESH:

4. Review Peter's encounter with an angel in Acts 12:1-11. Observe how many times current magazine articles refer to the ministry of angels and be ready to share with your study group any of these exciting reports.

Lesson Eleven

LOVING HIM

"Let us love one another, for love comes from God. Everyone who loves has been born of God and knows God...because God is love." 1 John 4:7,8

I. Review

    A. Righteousness in the sight of God is based not on our performance alone, but on faith in Jesus who has become "our righteousness" by His sacrifice on the cross.

       The sinful nature and the weakness of our flesh keep us from being perfect. When we fail, we have an advocate with the Father, the Lord Jesus. He always honors the truly repentant heart.

    B. God has provided everything we need to help us live righteously:
       -salvation through Jesus.
       -His indwelling Holy Spirit who guides and gives us strength.
       -the Holy Scriptures to show us how to live and to teach us of himself.
       -the church with its pastors, teachers, prophets, and evangelists.
       -the watchful care of angels who serve us.
       -Jesus as our intercessor.

II. The widow's lot in Naomi's day was one of sorrow and hardship. When she lost her husband, her source of support, guidance, and protection was gone. Often she knew real poverty.

A. In Moab, unless her family intervened, the only source of support for the widow was prostitution. But God was ready to fill Naomi and Ruth's lives with love and joy again. He forgives! He restores!

   Read: Ruth 4:13-16

B. God gives a special promise to the widow and detailed instructions for her care, both in the Old Testament law and in Paul's instructions to the church.

   Read: Deuteronomy 26:12; Psalm 68:5; 146:9; 1 Timothy 5:3-16

III. Without God it is impossible to know love. Love comes from God. In fact, God **is** love. In America we use the word *love* for everything from hamburgers to husbands, but the Greek language has several words to more clearly delineate the meaning of *love*.

   Read: 1 John 4:7,8

A. *EROS* - Physical, passionate, or sentimental love.

   Sexual desire, or temporary infatuation may be mistaken for love. All absorbing, desiring to possess, and motivated by impulse, *eros* is conditional. "I'll love you if..." Many individuals have been hurt and their lives ruined because sensual desire was mistaken for love.

However, romantic love (*eros*) can revitalize a marriage relationship. Ed Wheat, physician and certified sex therapist, emphasizes that romantic love can be a *learned response*.[11] As a partner consistently chooses to think on the favorable aspects of a spouse, and to respond with kindness and understanding, the emotion of romantic love grows. An exciting intimacy is developed that restores the joy of being together.

Certainly, anger and unforgiveness have to be laid aside if romantic love is to thrive. Criticism and harsh words create a barrier. Lack of respect for the other person destroys responsive love, because *eros* is conditional.

God has provided for a joyous sexual expression of love between husband and wife. We are commanded by Scripture to regularly meet the sexual needs of a spouse. To not do so is to defraud one's mate and to invite temptation.

Read: Proverbs 5:18,19; 1 Corinthians 7:2-5; Hebrews 13:4

B. *PHILEO* - Tender affection or brotherly love.

As thrilling as *eros* can be, it will not survive the pressure of everyday living unless it is sustained by another kind of love. *Phileo* speaks of a

---

[11]Ed Wheat, M.D., *Love Life for Every Married Couple* (Grand Rapids, MI: Zondervan Publishing House, 1980) p.87.

friendship that shares thoughts, feelings, and
dreams. It cherishes and enjoys the object of its
affection.

Sometimes *phileo* is used to describe the love of
the Father for the Son (John 3:35) and for the
believer (John 14:21), as well as Jesus' love for
John (John 13:23), but is never used in a command
to men to *love* God.[12]

Phileo, as *eros*, always expects a response and
therefore can change and fade. It is a conditional
expression of caring: "I love you because...you are
beautiful, warm, or kind. You make me feel good,
happy."

Share: *Have you ever experienced a friendship
that could be described by the definition of phileo?
It what ways was it good? What did it lack?*

C. *AGAPE* - describes God's love. It is unconditional.
It is unselfish. It makes no demand for a response.
Agape says, "I love you because I choose to. I love
you regardless of your faults or weaknesses."

Agape can mend a broken relationship because it
is offered by choice. It does not depend on the
response of the object. It focuses on what the
giver says and does, rather than on how he feels.

---

[12]W.E.Vine, *An Expository Dictionary of New Testament Words,*
(Fleming H. Revell Company, Old Tappan, NJ, 1966) pp.20-22.

It is a deliberate act, motivated by the welfare of the recipient.

God's love is seen in the gift of His Son to people who were entirely unworthy. While we were still in sin, He loved us.

Read: Romans 5:8; 1 John 4:9,10

Illustration: John 21:15-17
In His question to Peter, Jesus used the word agapao, *but Peter responded with* phileo, *emphasizing his personal affection for the Lord. In His third question, "Do you really love me?" Jesus changes to the word* phileo. *He is asking, "Since you cannot claim unconditional* agape, *do you really love me as a friend with all the fervor you are claiming?"* [13]

IV. God offers love as the "most excellent way" to live. His intent for the body of believers was, and is, that they work in harmony with one another.

   A. *Agape*'s qualities reflect the fruit of the Spirit as given in Galatians 5:22,23: joy, peace, patience, kindness, goodness, faithfulness, gentleness, and self-control.

   B. *Agape* rejoices when a brother or sister in the Lord succeeds. It is always kind and trusts that God has

---

[13]The Pulpit Commentary (Wilcox & Follett Co., Chicago, IL) Volume 40, p. 506.

arranged the parts of the body "just as He wanted them to be." It eliminates jealousy and competition and allows for one another's spiritual gifts and different levels of growth.

Read: 1 Corinthians 12:18; 13:1-13

C. God created us with the ability to give and receive love. However, the capacity to give love and to allow others to love us was diminished by the fall.

Read: John 14:15;21;23,24; 1 John 4:19-21

Often one's own needs are so great they get in the way of loving perfectly. When hurt by people, or when basic needs are not being met, a person may not be able to give unconditional love.

Every individual has basic needs:
-To be understood, accepted, and wanted.
-To feel secure and safe with needs like food and shelter provided in acceptable ways.
-To feel capable with something worthwhile to offer.
-To have personal value, the right to live.

Read: 1 Corinthians 14:1; 16:14

D. Love is demonstrated in many ways:

Examples:
The love of a mother for a child - giving a kidney to save its life; driving for hours to deliver the child to school, on a paper route, or to a friend's

house; cooking, cleaning, and serving even when tired. In sickness, when handicapped or wayward, a child is still loved by its mother.

The love of a faithful friend - accepting inconvenience for the sake of the other, sharing valuable time and energy to keep the friendship special, or perhaps risking health and life to care for the other.

The devotion of a husband and father - working day after day to provide for his family, giving his life to protect his children from danger, or sacrificing personal desires for those of the ones he loves.

God's love for His creation - shown by His care, protection, and provision; revealed in the beauty He brings us: flowers, music, blue sky, colors, calming water, cool breezes; and demonstrated by the peace and joy of His presence.

V. Jesus said that the greatest of all commandments is to "Love the Lord your God with all your heart and with all your soul and with all your mind." How is it possible for frail, fallible people to do this in a way that will please a holy, heavenly Father?

  A. John 14 lets us know that our love for God will be demonstrated by obedience. Regardless of what we might call "extenuating circumstances," pressures from family and culture, or undesirable results of our action, loving God demands absolute obedience.

Read: John 14:23,24; 15:10-13

Illustration:
Job determined to trust God no matter what happened to him. Though it looked as though God had deserted him, he continued to believe and trust in a God who was just and loving. He said, "Though he slay me, yet will I hope in him" (Job 13:15).

B. Loving God always results in loving one another. As believers live out their faith in a world of strife and trouble, they find purpose and hope. As they serve one another in love, they are a reflection of God.

VI. God made us in His own image. What He says about us is more important than what friends, parents, spouse, children, or our own thoughts tell us. He says we are *chosen, forgiven, loved,* and *bought with a price.* Nowhere else in the world will we find one who knows us completely and yet loves us unconditionally.

Read: Genesis 1:26; 1 Peter 1:18,19

God has provided the only way that we can find perfect, unconditional love. It is found in a personal relationship with the Lord Jesus. The one who knows and lives in the love of God, experiences a joy and peace none other can know. The Heavenly Father longs to teach us His ways and share with us His peace. We must allow Him to love us with His gentle, sacrificial love.

To Do at Home This Week:Lesson Eleven

1. No other author of Holy Scripture wrote as much about love as did John, "the beloved." What two things did John say reveal our love for God?

   John 14:23; 15:10; 1 John 2:5

   _____

   John 15:12; 1 John 4:7

   _____

2. God is able to help us change the way we feel about other people. John did not always act in loving ways at the beginning of his discipleship. In the following scriptures discover some of John's "before" actions:

   Mark 10:35-37_____

   _____

   Luke 9:51-56_____

   _____

3. Jesus teaches that it is easy to love those who love us, but as His disciples we are to go a step further and love our "enemies."

Can you identify the enemies in your life? This could be anyone who has hurt you, offended you, or makes life difficult in an ongoing way. Who are they?

What are some ways you could obey the Lord and demonstrate love to these individuals?

4. Have you ever tried "turning the other cheek"? What happened?

5. In what practical ways does God demonstrate His love for us in the following verses?

Psalm 145:15,16_____

Matthew 5:45_____

Acts 14:17_____

Lesson Twelve

SHARING HIM

"The man who plants and the man who waters have one purpose, and each will be rewarded according to his own labor." 1 Corinthians 3:8

I. Review

    A. God has provided the only Source for knowing perfect love (*agape*). In a personal relationship with the Lord Jesus, we begin to understand love that is unselfish and unconditional.

    B. God requires that we live in obedience to His commands. As the love fruit of the Spirit develops in our lives, we experience more patience, kindness, temperance, and faithfulness in our relationship to others.

II. We cannot live without affecting other people. The decisions we make will impact the people we know, especially those of our own families.

The news of Ruth and Naomi's return spread throughout Bethlehem (Ruth 1:19), and Boaz and Ruth's vows were witnessed by people of the town (4:11). But, their influence didn't stop there. The son they bore became the grandfather of King David and ancestor of the Lord Jesus Christ.

Read: Ruth 4:16-22

    A. The world around us, and the people in it, is a harvest field. Because of sin's curse, all the world

is under a death sentence. There will soon be six
billion people in the world. Every hour over 3,600
die and face their Creator in eternity.

Read: Matthew 7:14; Romans 3:23; 6:23

If the gospel of Jesus Christ is to be shared
effectively, the world, our friends, and family
members, must be seen as lost without Christ.
Regardless of how important they are, or how dear
to us, unless they know and accept God's plan of
salvation, they are headed for an eternity of
torment and suffering.

Read: John 3:16,17; 2 Thessalonians 1:8-10;
Revelation 20:15

B. It is easier to feel compassion for the physical
needs of people than for the less visible spiritual
needs. We want to help the deaf or blind. We
send flowers and visit those who are hurting. We
pray earnestly for physical healing for those who
are sick.

But the greater need for spiritual health is often
overlooked because people don't necessarily appear
spiritually ill. They may have everything they
need for a comfortable life. They may be busy,
and seemingly content or happy.

C. Clearly, our first mission field is wherever we live.
The disciples were instructed to share the gospel
"first in Jerusalem" (Acts 1:8), before they went to
distant lands.

The vision and effort of each Christian for evangelism must concentrate on the people touched in daily living. Those who are close at home and at work, and those whose activities bring them across our paths regularly, are the ones to whom we are under orders to bring the gospel.

In spite of repeated scriptural commands to take the message and make disciples, only one Christian in twenty will ever lead a soul to Christ. Perhaps the greatest hindrance to being witnesses for the Lord is personal pride and fear.

Read: Matthew 5:16; 28:19,20; 2 Timothy 1:8; Philemon 1:6

Share: How many people can you bring to mind whom you know are not acquainted with Jesus? How often do you see them? Make a list of these individuals and begin to pray now that God will give you opportunities to lead them to Him.

III. Becoming an effective witness for Christ requires that one's life and attitudes be right before God.

A. *A feeling of weakness, or discontent with one's own spiritual experience will limit the effectiveness of a witness.* The believer's experience must be personal and current, but the Gospel, shared even in weakness, is powerful. Christians should see themselves as forgiven, not perfect.

Read: 2 Corinthians 4:1; Philippians 4:13; 2 Timothy 1:7,12

B. *It is important to maintain good relationships within the body of Christ.* Anger or unforgiveness toward fellow Christians will come through in the way people talk about their faith. It is important to keep short accounts with other people so that bitterness does not develop.

Read: 1 Corinthians 1:10

C. *A Christian's attitude toward the unbeliever must be one of love and understanding.* He can ask God for wisdom in dealing with difficult people and know that the Lord is able to break down barriers. Not everyone will want to hear. Indeed, the message may be foolishness to them. But genuine caring can reach the hardest heart.

Sensitivity to an acceptable way of presenting the truth in the particular situation, as well as respect for the other person's time, pride, and beliefs is essential. Signs of openness or of antagonism and disinterest should be observed.

Read: 1 Corinthians 1:18; 1 Peter 4:14-16

D. *A witnessing person needs to believe that God wants to save, and that He is able to do so.* The Holy Spirit will do the convicting, drawing, and convincing. As the good news is shared, the seed can be watered with tears in prayer, but it is God who gives the increase and brings the seed to maturity.

Read: 1 Corinthians 3:6,7; 2 Peter 3:9

IV. Different kinds of witnessing are needed to reach the stranger, or close friends and members of the family.

A. *To strangers, new acquaintances or casual friends,* a personal testimony can be shared in a conversational way...a healing, a financial miracle, or the renewal of a relationship. Most effective is that which relates to the person and therefore interests them. Stories should be able to be documented, not be just hearsay. The conversation can be turned from the topic being discussed to spiritual things without being offensive, argumentative, or preachy.

Illustrations:
"Your children are so special to you. Have you given much thought to their training in spiritual matters?"

"I am really sorry to hear about (a death in the family, an illness, a wayward child). May I pray with you about this?"

"If someone were to ask you, 'What is a Christian?' what would you tell him?" (Church attendance, prayer, living a good life, etc. are things a Christian **does**, but what **is** he?)

Read: 2 Timothy 2:14,23,24; 1 Peter 3:15

B. *Witnessing to family members and close friends requires what we call "lifestyle evangelism."* Those who are close see what goes on in the daily grind. The most important thing is to live a consistent Christian life, with honest dealings, and without hidden, personal sin.

Discussing religion is rarely helpful and in fact, may be a hindrance. If there is to be a conversation about the Lord, it may be wise to let the unsaved friend or family member take the lead.

A readiness to share the positive things of the Lord without arguing or complaining about another Christian's failure, or about problems within the church, makes for a positive witness. The excitement and joy of knowing Christ should bubble over and permeate every facet of the Christian's life.

Read: 1 Timothy 4:16; Philippians 2:14,15; 1 Peter 3:1-4

V. When given an opportunity to share the gospel with a hungry heart, it is important to use the Word of God. The Word is powerful in itself. It is like a sword in the hand and needs to be used carefully, letting it do its own work.

The Word becomes more powerful when it has affected the life of the believer in a personal way. The Holy Spirit is faithful to bring to remembrance that which has been learned. As the Word convicts or encourages, it becomes a part of one's life, and is available to be used when needed in witnessing.

Read: John 14:26

A. A small New Testament, carried in pocket or purse, can be referred to and then given to the hearer as his own.

It is helpful to *have five key verses marked* to share in the following order: Romans 3:23, Romans 6:23, John 1:12, John 1:9, and Romans 10:9,10. At the bottom of each page, a tiny page number can be printed for the next verse so it can be turned to easily.

Sharing these verses is sowing seed. To bring the grain to harvest one more step is needed: the presentation of a key question. *"You can receive Jesus now. He wants to be your Savior and is knocking at the door of your heart. Won't you invite Him to come in and take control of your life?"* (See Revelation 3:20)

B. *A witness can be stopped at any point that resistance is felt.* Nothing is gained by forcing, alienating, or closing the door for future conversation. God allows for the free will of the individual. He does not force Himself upon the sinner but is faithful to bring other influences into his life to prod him towards salvation.

If the door is open, *the person can be invited to a special service or Christian activity* of interest to them.

C. *Follow-up prayer for the one being witnessed to* can help bring continued conviction. A prayer burden may be shared with another Christian with prudence, not giving personal information that might prove embarrassing if the individual comes to church later.

Read: 2 Corinthians 4:7

VI. It is not enough to give birth to a new baby. It must be cared for, fed, taught, and protected. New Christians must be discipled and taught step-by-step if they are to experience growth and come to maturity. Some things are absolutely essential to survival.

Read: Colossians 2:6,7; 1 Peter 2:2,3; 2 Peter 1:3,5-8

A. *Bible study, just like food, must be taken each day.* It is best to begin in the New Testament with the stories of Jesus. Have the new Christian mark any areas that need further explanation and ask these of the discipler at an appointed time.

Read: 2 Timothy 3:16

B. *The babe in Christ must practice times of prayer.* Prayer, simply talking to God and listening to Him, can take place at any time, in any place, in any position. A mature, committed Christian can model effective prayer for the inexperienced.

Read: Ephesians 6:18

C. *Church attendance is important to ongoing spiritual development.* Scriptural teaching and gifts are in operation for the benefit of the body of Christ and should be cultivated there.

Getting involved in one church, rather than going from group to group, helps eliminate confusion and allows for a more complete training process. Statistics tell us that in order to remain in a church, a person must form strong ties with 2 or 3 people and become acquainted with at least 10.

Read: Romans 12:3-8; 1 Corinthians 12:28

Christian fellowship helps build faith. The discipler should be a friend to the person he leads to the Lord. Sometimes old ties must be broken with those who would weaken the new Christian's walk with God.

Read: Ephesians 5:19-21

VII. Naomi's witness to Ruth must have been a very powerful one. Everything about this beautiful relationship speaks of careful discipleship and teaching. As a result of great love and commitment to each other, Ruth was enabled to leave her family, home, and friends and go with Naomi to Israel. There in the tangles of her life she found God.

To Do at Home This Week:Lesson Twelve

1. How important was a "witness" in a scriptural context?

    Deuteronomy 17:6; 19:15

2. What am I (as a Christian) a witness of?

    Acts 2:32

    Acts 5:32

    Acts 10:39

3. Where is a Christian to be a witness?

    Matthew 28:19 and Acts 1:8

    Share just what this means to you in terms of where
    and how you share the Lord.

4. What three things must a person be made aware of before he can really receive the good news?

   Romans 3:23

   Acts 16:31

   Romans 10:9, 10

5. To fulfill the Lord's commission to be a witness, name three people you know who do not know the Lord and begin now to pray for them and to think of ways to share the good news with them.